FARADAY

A community rediscovered

Robyn Howarth

Faraday
A community rediscovered

First published in Australia by Robyn Howarth 2024

Copyright © Robyn Howarth 2024
All Rights Reserved

A catalogue record for this
book is available from the
National Library of Australia

ISBN: 978-1-7635211-0-0 (pbk)
ISBN: 978-1-7635211-1-7 (ebk)

Typesetting and design by Publicious Book Publishing
Published with the assistance of Publicious Book Publishing
www.publicious.com.au

No part of this book may be reproduced in any form,
by photocopying or by any electronic or mechanical
means, including information storage or retrieval
systems, without permission in writing from both the
copyright owner and the publisher of this book.

Contents

Prologue i

1 January 1972 1
2 Farm Life 6
3 We are going to make a fortune 16
4 The joys of connected landline phones 18
5 Faraday Primary School 797 21
6 Remember the days of the old school yard?
   We used to laugh a lot 23
7 Politics and the importance of
   wearing gloves! 30
8 Ladies, a plate please? 35
9 A most evil plan is hatched 38
10 Shopping days in Castlemaine 40
11 Freezing Faraday, frozen pipes
   and cold feet 44
12 Enid Blyton and Hair 47
13 Bessie, the favourite cow 50
14 Evil was circling 52

15	So much to look forward to	55
16	The calm before the storm	58
17	Kidnapped	65
18	The long drive to who knows where	71
19	Deep in the bush	75
20	Mum's story	79
21	Consternation	83
22	The plan unravels	85
23	The story hits the press	88
24	Police investigation in Melbourne	91
25	Faraday and Castlemaine	94
26	The community rallies	96
27	The longest evening	98
28	Lone Pine Farm – 8.00 pm	103
29	D24 Melbourne - Police Headquarters	105
30	The escape	114
31	Chaos and confusion	121
32	Reunited	125
33	The police investigation	128
34	Catch those madmen	133
35	You can choose your friends, but not your relatives!	136
36	The line-up	142
37	One week after the kidnapping	145

38	Two weeks after the kidnapping............................. 147
39	Oh no, not Melbourne! 149
40	Detective Sergeant Reginald (Reg) Baker's story 152
41	Trial no. 1 - a blunt trauma 163
42	Reliving the crime over and over 167
43	Do not vomit.. 169
44	A good copper.. 172
45	Trial no. 2 - repeat blunt trauma............................. 177
46	The wife 180
47	Lois' story... 185
48	Trial no. 3 - repeated blunt trauma 190
49	Is it the end?... 193
50	Treading water... 195
51	Adulting... 204
52	Madness and mothering... 210
53	Finding peace and wisdom..................................... 216
54	Today. Castlemaine.. 218

End Notes 223
Notes on Sources.. 225
Appendix... 227

Prologue

Always the same dream. Always so real. The man—or is it a monster—looms over me, cruel eyes gleaming through the black balaclava. He slowly pulls the knife out from the brown overnight bag, brandishing it around, getting closer and closer.

He soon tires of this game. He then slowly draws the shotgun out of the bag, caressing it lovingly, and his eyes twinkle with mirth. He positions the shotgun snugly into his shoulder, takes aim and fires. I wake up screaming as I feel the bullet penetrate my heart.

My heart is pounding, my mouth is dry, I feel like I want to be sick. Another sleepless night.

It is only a dream, I keep repeating to myself, *it is only a dream.*

But I know evil is out there.

It found us at Faraday the day we were kidnapped.

I was only ten years old.

6 October 1972
They said they had nothing to gain from killing us—but nothing to lose either!

It was a scary feeling to have at ten years of age—to think this might be it, that life as you know it will be over, and we could all die.

PROLOGUE

I remember thinking, in a clumsy, innocent way, as the masked man with a sawn-off shotgun bundled us into the van, that this was not fair. I felt slightly aggrieved. I had not yet had a chance to live, but I also did not understand death yet either.

Present time
The nightmares have gone now. But it took a long time—years actually—and quite a bit of counselling. In the seventies, there was not a lot known about post-traumatic stress disorder (PTSD) and childhood trauma. But it was a journey I found myself navigating; and not always very well.

Going back in time to write this story has surprisingly given me a great deal of comfort to revisit the days of my childhood and mourn for those who are no longer with us. It has given me a chance to appreciate just how loved we were.

I have procrastinated long and hard that my writing is not good enough to tell the story I want to tell. Stories of farming, friendships, family, and Faraday, which have made me laugh and often cry. But after 1972, the only story ever told when Faraday was mentioned, was that of the Faraday School kidnapping.

Our life at Faraday was always so much more. And this is my story. My voice.

1
January 1972

We led a very simple life but I was very excited. I was going into Grade 5 and would be the oldest student in my school. We only had ten students but it was still pretty cool to be the oldest kid in the whole school.

These school holidays really dragged along. There were hot days where we would play under the sprinkler, the water pressure just a dribble, on the only strip of lawn in the front yard. Mum had planted some trees, but they were struggling and shade was scarce at best. Our small weatherboard home, located on the Calder Highway, was always hot in summer because the wood stove in the kitchen would be alight so that Mum could cook for her hungry family. Four growing daughters and a husband, two dogs, numerous cats, lots of chooks, a pony (Mandy), and an assortment of pet lambs and sheep generally hanging around the house. Poor Mum.

The land around our house was dry and parched, the tracks dusty, the creeks and dams had very little water, and there was sheep milling around in the mottled shade under the gum trees, trying to keep cool. The flies would continually enter via the flyscreen door leading onto

JANUARY 1972

our porch as pieces of flywire were loose and hanging off. Another job Dad hadn't gotten around to. We never enjoyed summer.

Grandma Howarth was always warning us that we were never to go near the dams, particularly the one behind our house. This was because on really hot days we were tempted to duck up to that dam, which usually had some water in it and it always looked cool and inviting. Grandma would say, 'That dam is deeper than a car and very dangerous' and she would spend a lot of time telling us never to go near the dams as we could drown. None of the adults in our world could swim so we mostly heeded the dire warnings. But on forty-plus degree days, it was tempting to disobey as we could all swim because Mum had made sure we all had swimming lessons.

The furthest we got was the creek, which was situated on the Bendigo side of our house. Cool running water would run through there—not deep—and there were large rocks we could sit on, peering down to see if we could find frogs. We didn't actually tell Grandma we spent quite a lot of time in the creek as it was not the very dangerous dam. We thought she should not mind, but it was best not to bring it to her attention.

I was sad that summer because Lassie had died. Lassie was our beautiful black and white border collie. She was a sweet natured girl with a very stubborn streak. Dad had paid a lot of money for her as a puppy, which was unusual for him to do. She was also from a successful line of working dogs. I would overhear him bragging to the neighbours that his life would be so much easier now with his expensive, intelligent working dog. Unfortunately for Lassie though, he was a terrible dog trainer. His version of training seemed to consist of a lot of yelling and swearing. When that didn't work, he yelled louder and swore more. And Lassie was sensitive and didn't respond well to Dad's dog training style. She would simply ignore him when he yelled at her.

One day, Dad had enough of being ignored by Lassie and he gave her a smack. He always claimed that it was not a hard smack. But Lassie stared mournfully at him then turned away and trotted across several paddocks until she arrived home to her kennel, where she lay down and refused to come out for the rest of the day. The next day however, Lassie seemed to have forgiven Dad and they went off to work around the farm as usual. But when Dad gave her a command to round up the sheep, she sat down, turning her head and refusing to look at him. He gave her the same command but in a louder voice this time. Lassie looked sadly at him before taking herself home and staying in her kennel for the rest of the day.

This happened the next day and then the next … well forever really. Dad would say to us all, 'Bugger me, that dog, I only gave her a tap. That's it, no more female dogs, they are just too bloody temperamental.'

I always felt a little sorry for Dad and Lassie as they were an ill-matched pair—a sensitive dog with a stubborn streak, and a farmer with little skill in dog training. But Lassie was his girl right to the end.

This became the pattern. Dad and Lassie would go off to work together every morning at the same time. And Lassie would spend the day turning her back on Dad after he gave her a command and sit staring in the opposite direction. During the course of the day, Lassie would usually come home alone. Mum always said she never forgave Dad for smacking her. We would see Lassie coming home and would call out, 'Mum, Mum, Lassie's home, Dad must have yelled at her again.'

There was a bond of affection between them as Lassie would happily follow Dad all over the farm. And there was never any talk of having her put down. But then … exciting news! Lassie was having puppies. We had no idea who the father was, but we were very excited for Lassie. Dad was hopeful that he might get a good working dog from one of the puppies—preferably a boy. He thought he would have better luck with a boy.

Lassie went into labour and laboured for a very long time. She had twelve puppies—a mixture of boys and girls. We were so excited, but Mum and Dad weren't. Their faces were very grim and they both looked sad. Lassie was just lying in her makeshift bed in the laundry, not moving and unable to lick her puppies. Lassie was sick and she died. Dad said having twelve puppies was just too much for her.

Mum would always have the wood fire stove burning, even in summer. After Lassie died, all the puppies were in a cardboard box against the brick wall in the laundry, which backed onto the wood stove. It provided some warmth for the puppies. We tried to feed them milk, but they were too little and frail. Each morning we would run out to the laundry to check on the puppies, only to find that each day there were fewer puppies in the box. The smaller puppies had died in the night. After a few days, there were three good sized puppies left and they were taking small amounts of milk. We were hopeful that these three would make it.

One by one they developed dreadful diarrhoea and finally there was one left—a little boy. He had no mother, and no brothers or sisters. He was black and tan, and he was soft, sweet and cuddly. I would say my prayers every night, 'Please let him live.' But sadly, it was not to be. That morning, I sat touching the warm bricks in the laundry and peered into the empty card box and cried.

It was not a good start to 1972. And there was worse to come.

2

Farm Life

Faraday was a small, untouched, pretty hamlet, seventy-one miles north of Melbourne—or as the locals referred to it, the big smoke. The land was fertile, with usually good rainfall, and the local farming families had farmed their land with pride for many generations. Nestled in the shadow of Mount Alexander, was our farm, 'Lone Pine', named after that solitary tree in Gallipoli. Our farm was very picturesque, complete with all sorts of animals—draft horses, pigs, sheep, cattle, and working dogs. Mother cats would have their kittens in the haystack. We always loved trying to find the kittens and would then beg Mum for yet another one. Our farm straddled both sides of the Calder Highway, with our homes situated on the eastern side of the road. The signpost that read, '71 miles to Melbourne' was our marker. It was located on the highway outside our front gate.

Grandma Howarth and Joe (Dad's younger, perennially bachelor brother), lived across the paddock in a large, red brick homestead with verandahs all around. It was surrounded by a lovely garden. We loved playing in Grandma's garden. It was so very lush compared to ours—

filled with geraniums, fuchsias and roses. Of particular delight was popping all the fuchsia buds, much to Grandma's annoyance, and eating the mulberries from the laden mulberry tree. We would get red mulberry juice all over our hands, faces and summer dresses, much to Mum's annoyance. We—and by we, I mean Mum (Iris), Dad (Rex), myself (Robyn, aged 10), Jill (aged 7), Denise (aged 5), and Suzanne (aged 3)—lived in a much smaller weatherboard home. Our garden was not lush as there seemed to always be problems with our water supply. We learned as children, and later as adults, to never mention the water pump as Dad would get very cranky. It was a very touchy subject.

He did seem to spend an inordinate amount of time fixing the water pump over the years, but water pressure never seemed to improve and our garden always struggled with a lack of water.

The Howarth family had farmed here since 1869, and we were the fourth generation of Howarths who attended Faraday State School. We were really proud to live in Faraday and attend the local primary school. We thought it was the best school in the world. My great-great-grandfather, James Howarth, was born in Lancashire, England in 1835, and migrated to Australia and settled on the fertile farming land at Faraday. At twenty-eight years of age, he married Alice Taylor, who was also born in Lancashire. She had been widowed and already had two children at the time of their marriage in Castlemaine in 1864. James and Alice went on to have seven children, two of whom died as infants and one who died as a teenager. The surviving two sons and two daughters all married Broads from Sutton Grange—not an uncommon occurrence among early pioneering families.

My great-grandfather, James Junior, who was one of the sons, continued the farming tradition at Faraday. He married twenty-one-year-old Emily Broad from Sutton Grange in 1899, and they went on to have three children, two of whom were boys—Leslie James and Walter John.

Sadly, James Junior died of pneumonia in Chewton in 1905 at the young age of thirty-three. He had only been married for six years and left behind a young widow and three small children. Emily went on to marry Tom Salathiel, a young man belonging to another well-known pioneering family in Faraday, and together they had three sons. My great-aunt, Clare Salathiel, aged to a spritely 104 years old and, at the time of writing this book, she still lived in their original blue stone cottage at Faraday.

My grandfather was Leslie James Howarth and he married Violet Louise Talbot from Taradale, Castlemaine in December 1922. They carried on farming at Faraday, successfully raising sheep and dairy cattle. They also tended an apple and pear orchard. They had six children—three sons and three daughters—and very early on, their career paths were mapped out. The decision was made that two of their six children would be allowed to leave the farm and pursue careers of their own choosing. The other four would be needed to work the family farm.

Lorraine (Lorrie), the eldest daughter, worked on the farm until her marriage to Roy Portwine, a local builder. They went on to have two daughters, Jenny and Linda, whom they raised in Castlemaine. They lived in a variety of lovely homes around the Castlemaine area. They were all built by Roy, whom Dad always fondly referred to as

Porty. Jim (James), the eldest son and Grandma's favourite (according to Dad), pursued a career in the PMG and was also a radio operator in the Second World War.

He had a very happy marriage to Lorna and they settled in Castlemaine and raised two daughters, Val and Ros.

Sadly, in November 1971, Jim collapsed and died of a heart attack at forty-four years of age. I remember the night Uncle Jim died. Family members gathered in Grandma's kitchen, all shocked and at a loss as to how could this happen to Jim, who was in the prime of his life. Grandma was in her usual seat adjacent the open fireplace, no emotion on her face, not speaking and dry eyed, staring resolutely towards the window. But she was clutching her cardigan so tightly around her body.

Uncle Jim would visit Grandma quite regularly on a weekend, always bringing her a lovely bunch of flowers. Grandma would proudly display the flowers in the kitchen and loved telling Dad for many days after what a thoughtful son Jim was.

Mum also would comment and say how charming and thoughtful it was that Jim always gave his mother flowers. Dad would usually get a bit disgruntled after that and mutter that he was too bloody busy working the farm to buy anyone flowers. He got over his fit of pique pretty quickly, until the next weekend when Jim visited again with more flowers.

Dad (Rex) was the third child and second son and farming would be his career. Dad never wanted to be a farmer and would have liked to get an apprenticeship as a builder, but that was never an option for him. He left school at fourteen years of age and commenced work on the family farm.

Ailsa was the fourth child, second daughter. She was a vivacious, confident personality and decided she would like to get into nursing. Her parents agreed and she embarked on her nursing career and married Russell McClure. Dad would always refer to Russell as Rusty. He moved away from the Faraday area and raised three daughters—Janet, Carol and Heather. Dad always had a soft spot for Ailsa because growing up they were close in age and would ride their ponies around the hills on the farm. They spent long hours exploring together.

June was the fifth child, the youngest daughter, best friend to Mum, my godmother, and one of the kindest people I ever knew. We all still mourn her to this day.

Auntie June desperately wanted to pursue a career nursing as well, but it was not to be. She also left school early and would work on the farm until her marriage to Dave Hoare, a local mechanic. They set up home in Castlemaine and raised two daughters—Annette and Wendy. After she was widowed in her fifties, she obtained employment at the local Castlemaine Hospital. She loved talking to the nursing staff and would often wistfully remark that she would have loved to have been a nurse.

Lester (Joe), the youngest of the tribe, struggled socially, never married and lived at home with his mother. He also worked the farm.

In retrospect, this was a good career path for him as he was surrounded by family and did have some good skills in animal husbandry.

Lassie, the border collie, was partial to Joe and would happily round up sheep all day with him and Dad—as long as it was Joe giving the commands.

We were a very female dominated family. Grandma

Howarth ended up with thirteen granddaughters. My grandfather collapsed and died suddenly and unexpectedly on Christmas Eve 1952. He had a heart attack and was only fifty-one years old. My father, Rex, was only twenty-one and was subsequently expected to step up and take charge of the family farm and be responsible for his mother and younger siblings. Christmas in 1952 was horrific for the family. Christmas day was spent in grief and planning a funeral.

A glowing testimony appeared in the Castlemaine Mail, the local paper, shortly after my grandfather's death.

> *Lesley James Howarth came from one of the best known and most respected local pioneering families, and had spent all his life in the district. His capacity for toil and willing service were a byword and his neighbourhood will always remember his timely help with seasonal and emergency problems. As a farmer, he was successful and unceasing in his moves for progress and he built up a very fine property and homestead and with his wife, who is a member of the well-known and highly esteemed Talbot family of Elphinstone, and with his family of three sons and three daughters, all of whom are held in popular esteem and high regard, the activities of dairying, orchard and sheep raising were maintained with enthusiasm and marked success.*
>
> *Their loyalty and support for all community efforts have always been readily available and the community will mourn with sorrow and keen regret this popular and much-loved citizen and the heartfelt*

sympathy of all will be extended to Mrs Howarth and the family in their great loss.

The funeral, which took place on Friday morning, was one of the largest seen in the district when a lengthy cortege of about 100 cars followed from the residence at Faraday to the Taradale cemetery. The wealth and beauty of the floral tributes received bore testimony of deep sense of public loss sustained at his death.

Special floral tributes were received from the Faraday Methodist Church, the Faraday school committee of which Mr Howarth was secretary and school correspondent for many years, and the Directors and Shareholders of the Harcourt Fruit Supply.

I, of course, never knew my grandfather. But people over the years described him as a larger-than-life character, who was dark haired, brown eyed and a very tall farmer, who loved to be out and about chatting to neighbours. He was also said to be involved in community life. Grandma Howarth was the complete opposite—a small, blonde-haired, blue-eyed woman, with a quiet and serious demeanour.

After 1952, Dad would dread Christmas every year—in particular Christmas Eve—and was always on edge until Christmas was over. He was usually quite short tempered in the days leading up to Christmas, and we would nag him each day about getting us a Christmas tree. Every year he would cut a branch from a pine tree for us. He would eventually come home, usually on Christmas Eve, with the pine tree branch and we would excitedly decorate it. The smell of pine tree would permeate the house and it would finally feel like Christmas. Dad was always very reluctant to join in with any enthusiasm with Christmas plans, but he would always start to relax and appeared to enjoy himself during the afternoon of Christmas Day.

It is only as I write this as an adult that I finally realise he was waiting for a catastrophe each Christmas Eve. He dreaded the day but did not have the words or emotional makeup to understand that. He dealt with it the only way he knew how—by not really dealing with it.

At the age of thirty-one, Dad married Iris McInnes (my mother) from Big Hill, Bendigo after a shy tortuous courtship—on Dad's side anyway. Dad was a very shy man back then. He was slightly built and from the age of fourteen, when he left school, his life consisted of hard manual labour on the farm. The responsibilities of the farm and the long hours did not leave much room for socialization or any hobbies, which led to limited social interactions. Dad was not a drinker so visiting the local pub was not an option and anyway, Faraday did not have a local pub. He had never joined any sporting clubs as his father always had work for him to do on weekends, and he continued that work ethic after his father's death. However, he did join Young Farmers with his younger sister, June, and as a result of this, he and June started attending local old-time dances.

June was always the life of the party. She had many friends, as opposed to her painfully shy older brother, and she struck up a friendship with two pretty young women—Iris and Janet McInnes, identical twins from Big Hill. This group started meeting up regularly at the dances, and the twins would always be dressed in matching long, pastel, organza dresses, with matching clutch bags and hair clips. They caused quite a stir at the local dances as they were mirror images of each other. June soon cottoned on that Dad (Rex) was quite keen on Mum (Iris) as he would stare forlornly at her from a corner in the distance. He would be dressed in his best suit—his only suit—and would spend ages before each dance furiously polishing his dance shoes.

June would be for ever nudging her brother to 'go and ask Iris for a dance'. He would eventually do this as he would get sick of his sister's nagging, but once the dance began, he became hopelessly tongue tied, so conversation was very limited. After months of attending the local dances with her older brother mooching about and trying to summon the courage to ask Iris out, June decided she needed to play Cupid. One particular night at the Lockwood Dance, the McInnes twins were having their usual lovely time, dancing with any young man who asked them. Rex was in his usual customary place in the corner, staring gloomily at his newly polished dance shoes.

June took it upon herself to organise how each of the women would get home. Naturally, Iris and Janet were always in the group that went home Bendigo way. June innocently told Iris that she had all the rides sorted for home. Iris thought nothing of this and went and collected her belongings, assuming she would be going home with her sister, Janet, as usual. Although she did think it was a little odd that June asked her to wait around the side of the hall instead of out the front.

June went and ordered her brother, Rex, to get the car and bring it around the side. She said she was tired and needed to go home as she had a headache. Rex, as usual, did what he was told and pulled up at the side and there was Iris waiting by herself. As he pulled up, June emerged from the doorway, dragged Iris to the car, pushed her in the front passenger side, and shut the door with a loud bang. She then bellowed to her brother, 'Take Iris home now!' and quickly ran back inside the hall. The plan worked as they went on to have a very successful courtship and they eventually married. I never found out how the rest of the group got home that night, including June and Janet.

3

We are going to make a fortune

Summer 1972

Saturday night was always a highlight for us. We would all gather around the large black and white TV in the lounge room, and watch *The Penthouse Club*, a variety show with Mary Hardy. And there was live crosses to the trots. We all thought Mary Hardy was so funny and loved watching the beautiful horses racing around the track at Moonee Valley in Melbourne. Dad loved the trots. Occasionally we would even go to a race at Moonee Valley, which was very exciting for us.

That summer we all entered a competition to win a trotter. It was run by *The Penthouse Club*. We had to submit a name for a horse, and if our name was chosen, the horse would be ours. Dad reckoned we had a really good chance of winning. We spent hours working out names, making lists, crossing out names, and adding new ones. We were certain we were going to win a racing trotter. What we were going to *do* with a racing trotter none of us, including Dad, had given much thought to. My choice of name was Robbie's Rogue. Jill chose Jill's Gentleman, Denise went with Denny's Pride, and Suzanne was too little to choose, so Dad picked Sue's

Pet for her. And if you are all wondering, no we never won the racehorse. And if we *had* won it, we did not have anywhere to house said horse. Dad said he couldn't understand it because the names we chose were really good. He decided the whole thing must have been rigged, so that what's we thought as well.

Dad worked very hard and each season had its own rewards and challenges, but we were poor. Our farm was not large and with two families living off of it, money was always very tight. Summer was a particularly busy time as we were always on high alert for bush fires and could not leave the farm. The grass would be tinder dry, the dams nearly empty and our weatherboard house too. It was like a furnace. Dad was always on edge in summer, and we were all taught to carefully watch out for any smoke on the horizon.

Dad would have his water tank loaded onto the back of his ute, ready to go to the assistance of any neighbours if a fire should break out. There was no fire brigade at Faraday. A call would come through on those stinking hot summer days, and Dad and Joe would run for the ute and take off to where they were needed. The neighbours would always do the same for us. It was an unwritten code of the bush—neighbours helping each other.

4
The joys of connected landline phones

Two short rings and a long ring, or a long ring followed by two short rings. Which was it? Telephones in the seventies were on a party line, with a receptionist at the exchange. While it was exciting to have a telephone, it had its challenges. Especially when it was connected to Grandma's line. Mum was a long-suffering daughter-in-law. Grandma Howarth was a formidable woman. She birthed six children, was widowed at a young age, was a true matriarch of the Howarth clan, and she loved the farm with a passion.

Our phone lines were connected to each other via the exchange and the way to distinguish was two short rings then a long ring. This was our call, and one long ring followed by two short rings was Grandma's. It took a little while to get the hang of it. So, it was always absolute quiet when the phone would ring. We would all listen very intently to work out whose call it was. We mastered this skill much more quickly than Grandma.

One evening after tea, I was in my usual place near the door, eavesdropping on Mum and Dad's nightly conversation. Mum started in a very exasperated tone.

'Rex. It is really getting too much. Your mother is listening in to all my phone calls.' Dad replied in an equally exasperated tone, 'I have talked to Mum and she says she isn't, but she did comment the other day that you do spend a lot of time talking to June about *Days of our Lives*.' Mum said, 'See what I mean? She is listening in and I can hear her breathing on the other end of the phone.' Dad said, 'No, she isn't really listening in. Just sometimes she gets confused with the rings.' Mum responded with, 'So then, Rex, why doesn't she hang up when she realises it's not her call?' Dad mumbled something I couldn't quite hear.

And then the conversation got even more interesting. 'And another thing, Rex, said Mum, 'It's ridiculous that every time your brother goes out to a dance, I have to get the girls ready. We all have to walk over the paddock and stay the night with your mother. For goodness sake, he is always home before midnight.' Dad said, 'Now, Iris. We have been through this before, my mother is very frightened that she will collapse and die one night if she is on her own.' Mum, in huffy voice, said, 'Well, then you can go over and sit with your mother until midnight and make sure she stays alive, even though she is as fit as a mallee bull.' Dad, in a strangled tone this time, said, 'Iris, you know I have suggested this many times, but Mum (Grandma) is adamant that she would be too worried about you and the girls as she is convinced that someone may break in and murder you all if I was not there to protect you. So, we all have to be together.' My ears really pricked up at this. I wonder who is lurking around that might murder us. As far as I knew, Faraday had no murders or crimes of any description. *More listening at doorways is needed*, I thought to myself.

As an adult, reflecting back, I am struck that with Grandma Howarth still waters ran very deep, disguising a deep-seated anxiety. While struggling to show emotion like her son, Rex, our dad, she would demonstrate her care in other ways.

One of my earliest childhood memories is sitting on Grandma's knee as a two year old, dreadfully sick with measles. Mum was away in hospital, giving birth to Jill. I still remember sitting on Grandma's knee, next to the open fire. My throat felt like it was on fire and I felt so sick and thirsty. I would snuggle into her chest and feel the woollen cardigan against my cheek. With her arms around me, she would gently rock me and give me sips of water. As I dropped off to sleep next to the open fire, I would continually wake, crying for my mum. She did this both day and night. It was a safe place nestled against her cardigan and in her arms.

And then, ten years later, it was my first day at secondary school. I was very nervously standing on the side of the Calder Highway, waiting to catch the school bus into Castlemaine. It was my first time travelling on a bus to get to school. So very nervous and so unsure of what high school would bring, I continually looked down the highway for the first sight of the school bus. I was worried about where I would sit, what I would say to the bus driver and worried I would trip getting on the bus—all the typical fears of an adolescent. Later that afternoon, Grandma told me I stood there for thirteen minutes before the bus came along. I then realised that Grandma had stood at her kitchen window, where she had a view of the highway, and waited and watched out for the bus with me.

5

Faraday Primary School 797

I started school at Faraday in 1967 and there were two other little girls in my grade—Christine Ellery and Leanne Carr. This was considered a really big grade for our little school and it was quite unheard of to have three students in the same grade. Both Christine and Leanne were the youngest of their families. They were petite, blonde little girls.

I was always tall for my age. I had blue eyes with long, brown hair and a spattering of freckles across my face. I always felt a little clumsy and awkward next to my smaller classmates.

I generally looked forward to going back to school as the summer school holidays always seemed to drag for me. Leanne and her family always went to the beach at Apollo Bay. We were so envious of them having a holiday at the beach. We would often ask Mum why we couldn't go to the beach. We never went anywhere. The answer was always the same, 'Your father cannot leave the farm at the height of bush fire season.' I was hoping that the Carr family had forgiven me as I had had a mishap with Murray, Leanne's older brother. The previous year, he went off to secondary school minus a front tooth—courtesy of me. It was a normal school day and during the lunch break Murray decided he would play bushrangers. He was running around with the lid of a metal rubbish bin held up in front of his face and was asking all the kids to punch the lid, pretending to be Ned Kelly. Being a lot younger, I was really happy to be included in his game, so when he told me to hit the lid, I did so with all my might and with a closed fist. The edge of the lid hit Murray in the mouth, knocking out his top front tooth.

For the afternoon's activities, the teacher at the time thought it would be a fun activity for us all to search for Murray's missing front tooth in the school ground. The teacher was impressed that I had knocked Murray's tooth out. Murray looked miserable and kept saying his mum would kill him. The other kids thought it was great that we got out of schoolwork to search for the missing tooth, and I was embarrassed and wanted the ground to swallow me up. When I got home, I confessed what I had done. I felt really bad. Dad said if he was stupid enough to walk around with a rubbish bin lid in front of his face asking kids to hit him, then he deserved to lose his tooth. Mum said, 'Next time he asks you to hit him, just walk off.' I worried for a long time about Murray and his missing front tooth. He never did ask me to hit him again and he told me that playing bush rangers with me was no fun at all. He must have forgiven me though as we remain close friends to this day.

6

Remember the days of the old school yard? We used to laugh a lot.

Our school was really pretty with its granite exterior and well-tended gardens surrounding the school building. Set back from the Calder Highway, it could hardly be seen from the road. For relief from the scorching summer heat, the windows of the school facing the Faraday/Chewton Road had been bricked up in 1908. This meant we never had any warning when visitors or parents would visit the school. This was a rare occurrence anyway but it was a factor in events to follow.

Our school grounds were really big. There was lots of room to run and play hide-and-seek. At the back of the school was the play equipment, consisting of monkey bars and swings. It was always an enjoyable pastime on a sunny day to hang upside down on the monkey bars and gaze up at the sky.

Trees lined the perimeter of the school ground. A shelter shed was adjacent to the school on the left-hand side. A single boys' toilet and a single girls' toilet were set on the northern side of the grounds. They were situated well apart and quite a long way from the school, or so it seemed on cold, rainy days. A large, old cypress tree grew in the corner adjacent the Calder Highway and had seats underneath surrounding the trunk. It was a good place to sit and eat lunch on hot days.

There was also an asphalted area directly in front of the school with a flagpole, where we would raise the Australian flag every Monday morning. It was an important job to be chosen to be the flag monitor. They were large grounds for a small number of children. There were trees to climb and lots of hidey holes behind bushes and gum trees. A large expanse of grassed areas also surrounded the school building. In spring we would sit among the grass and make daisy chains. We would pick and eat small, sweet green buds, which we called 'yum yums'. And they were delicious.

It was an exciting time for the Howarths in 1972 as there would be three Howarths at Faraday Primary School. We made up nearly a third of the school's enrolment. Jill would be entering Grade 3. She was the only student in that grade and was not really looking forward to the school year as she much preferred being home on the farm and looking after the farm animals. Our younger sister, Denise, who would be five in the March, was starting prep. She would be the only student in her grade too. Denise was a very tiny, blonde-haired girl, whose school bag was nearly as big as she was.

Each morning we would climb up the steps at the front of the school with our school bags and enter the front door, which led to a small entry/porch area. There we would hang up our bags and enter through another door into the one-roomed main classroom. Denise was always struggling to reach her peg. The teacher's desk was in the corner along the back wall of the room. To our right was the large blackboard and facing the blackboard were ten desks neatly set out. Ten desks was a huge number for Faraday because two new families had moved into the area, causing an increase in enrolments to ten children and five families that year.

The youngest children would sit closest to the board, while the older students were towards the back of the room. There was a timber floor, which was always good for sliding on in our socks when we had to play games indoors and the teacher let us take our shoes off.

Christine, Leanne and I would all be in Grade 5 and would be the seniors in the school. We were quite chuffed about that. Christine was on track to win the Old Boys' prize the following year in Grade 6. This was for academic excellence. She was a very smart girl, who was also pretty gifted. She had large, blue eyes and thick blonde hair. I was always a little envious as she was the cleverest student in our school, but more importantly her family owned quite a few exotic dogs—well, exotic by Faraday standards. I would often nag Mum about visiting the Ellerys to look at their new puppies. They were Pomeranians and Papillons—adorable little fluff balls and dearly loved family pets.

Of course, as soon as I got home, I would start nagging Mum and Dad for a puppy like the Ellerys had. Dad would just mutter, 'Hmph! don't know what Charlie Ellery (father to Christine) is thinking. Those sorts of dogs will be no use chasing the bloody sheep.'

Leanne was our nearest neighbour and lived on the opposite side of the Calder Highway, one mile north of our home. Leanne was a very tiny, blonde girl with freckles on her nose. She had a great love of animals. One of the happiest days of her life was when she got her first pony—a beautiful boy named Ben, who was with her until he left this world at the ripe of age of thirty.

Leanne and Ben would often be seen out and about on weekends and school holidays, taking long rides together. They were both totally in tune with each other. The tiny, blonde-haired girl with rider's helmet secured and a beaming smile in place, rode her dappled grey pony with a lustrous mane. She would happily trot around exploring the delights of Faraday by horseback. It was their favourite thing to do.

The other students were Linda and Helen Conn. Linda was going into Grade 4. She was a quiet, studious young girl with short, dark, curly hair and large expressive brown eyes. She was conscious to always do the right thing. One day in the previous school year in the early afternoon, she had tentatively approached the male teacher at the time and said in her quiet voice, 'Sir, I have finished the schoolwork you have set me. What would you like me to do now?' The male teacher, in a joking voice, said, 'Wow, that was quick. Well, best go home then.' Linda lived quite a few miles from the school. Sometime later, the teacher looked around and asked, 'Where is Linda?' Someone piped up, 'She went home, sir.' The teacher ran outside and saw Linda struggling up the side of the Calder Highway with her school bag, on her way home. At that stage, he became a little agitated and red faced and ran across the school grounds to the fence adjacent the Calder Highway yelling, 'Linda, come back. It was a joke, Linda. It's not home time yet.'

Helen, entering Grade 1, was quite a contrast in appearance to her older sister. She had blonde hair with blue eyes and a lively, excitable personality. She seemed thrilled to be at school and thrilled to be learning and would listen very attentively to Miss Gibbs.

The two new families that caused a lot of excitement were quite a novelty in Faraday terms anyway. Terry and Richard Lord, who were entering Grade 4 and Grade 3, had recently emigrated from England with their very jolly parents and lots of older brothers and sisters. They had rented a farmhouse and it was obvious that money was tight. The house they had found was quite run down and the car they drove was very old.

But the whole family radiated such good humour and enthusiasm, and that Easter Terry and Richard proudly gave each of us and Miss Gibbs an Easter egg. I was really touched by this.

Lastly, Tracey Doyle was also in Grade 1. Her dad was a jockey, which was a very exciting career for the Faraday community. Tracey struggled a little. Initially, being in a new school, she always found it hard to say goodbye to her mum each day and took a while to settle each morning. Her mum would often come back at lunch time with her lunch. We were a school of eight girls, two boys, six families—and none of us were wealthy.

All of us were delivered to school and collected each day in the family cars. Even though we only lived approximately a mile from the school, Mum and Dad had decided it was far too dangerous to walk to school along the Calder Highway as we might get run over.

Every year we would have a new teacher. The teachers only ever stayed for one year. I guess being sent to a one-teacher school in rural Victoria was not the most prized teaching position. At the start of each school year, parents and students were always very keen to know who the new teacher would be. We, the kids, just hoped for a nice teacher. The parents hoped for one that might stay longer than one year.

Our new teacher for 1972, we found out, was a young woman whose name was Mary Gibbs. We found out via Mrs Conn, who knew someone, who knew someone else, who was related to the Gibbs family. News travelled fast in a small rural community. She was twenty years of age and this was her first school as a trained teacher. She would drive down each day from Bendigo, where she still lived at home with her parents. We all thought it was such a long way, all of twenty-two miles. There were mutterings between the fathers, who were all on school council, about whether some local accommodation could be found as driving back and forward from Bendigo each day was unheard of. This was a trip you only did once a week if that.

Our first impression of our new young teacher was that she was very pretty. She had dark-coloured hair and beautiful clothes. Our mothers thought she was so stylish with shortish skirts and amazing high heel shoes. I think the fathers did too. She was also quite strict and made sure we followed the timetable she had set, which consisted of Maths, English, Social Studies, Science, Sport, Music, and Religious Instruction.

Religious Instruction was delivered by a very sweet elderly couple. They would visit our school complete with a collapsible organ, which they would set up and then play, very loudly, 'Onward Christian Soldiers'. We were all really fascinated by that organ and sang 'Onward Christian Soldiers' with gusto and enthusiasm, but we were very off key. It was one of my favourite lessons. We did try and be helpful when we saw the couple arrive, struggling through the door with their organ, red faced and breathless. We would run over and try and help drag the organ into the room.

7
Politics and the importance of wearing gloves!

Faraday – March 1972

Times were a changing! A great deal of social change was occurring and that even found its way to sleepy Faraday. It was the year that Gough Whitlam and the Labour Party came to power on the back of the very successful 'It's Time' campaign. There was a lot of talk around the kitchen table about Gough and the Labor Party that year. Mum thought he delivered wonderful speeches. Dad would say voting for the National Party was a waste of time. He would say, 'They are as useless as tits on a bull, so you may as well vote for the Libs, and they are only for the rich, so bugger that. So, this Gough fellow seems to know what he is talking about. Clever bastard really. A barrister, I think, Iris. I think we should vote Labor this election.' Mum thought that was a good idea and commented again about the wonderful speeches Mr Whitlam gave.

We would head off on our weekly Sunday drive up to Big Hill to see Grandma and Grandpa McInnes (Bill and Marjorie McInnes, my maternal grandparents). It was a visit that was usually very calm—but not that weekend. Grandpa and Grandma McInnes were a little more affluent than the Howarth side and owned a small farm in Big Hill just outside Bendigo.

Their home was a lovely sprawling homestead with wide verandahs all the way around. There was a neatly clipped hedge at the front of the home, adjacent a good sized lawn—just the right size for grandchildren to run and somersault. On the northern side of the house was a very large vegetable garden with an array of fresh produce and delicious tasting strawberries we would pick when Grandma wasn't looking.

On very hot days, Grandpa would let us go down to the cellar that was located under the house off the verandah. We would enter through a secret door and climb down the steps. The cool air would hit us instantly. It was a large cellar, very dark and somewhat damp, and I was always hoping I would find hidden treasure. But alas, I never did.

Grandma McInnes would make us homemade icy poles to eat, and there would always be a delicious afternoon tea with homemade biscuits, cream sponge and sandwiches. Sometimes after afternoon tea, Grandma would let us explore the front bedrooms that had been Mum and her sisters' rooms. Mum was one of four girls, with her older sister, June; twin sister, Janet; and younger sister, Lorraine. They had all married and had long left home.

Grandma had kept their beautiful ball gowns still hanging in their wardrobes. They were all different coloured long gowns from vibrant burgundy to pale pinks and lilac with lace and tulle. Some were decorated with small, embroidered flowers and had hoop skirts. I thought they were the most beautiful gowns I had ever seen. During some visits, Grandma even let us try them on.

Grandpa was a farmer too and even though his farm was small, it was very profitable. Grandma was a midwife, although she did not continue her nursing career after her marriage. Grandma McInnes actually delivered her son-in-law (Dad) as she had been working as a midwife in Castlemaine and was on duty the day Dad was born.

The family story that was told to me was Grandma's (Marjorie) father, Moses Salathiel, raised his large family at Sutton Grange on a magnificent property known as Fairbank, now home to the iconic Sutton Grange Winery. He was a very strict father. Moses had twelve children, including quite a few daughters, and he took an instant dislike to any prospective suitors, Grandpa McInnes (Bill) included. He would ban them from setting foot on Fairbank.

Marjorie was a bright ambitious young woman and decided to pursue a career in nursing before specialising in midwifery. Marjorie was able to convince her father, Moses, that she needed to move to Melbourne to complete her studies. And there was precedent for this as her older sister, Stella, had recently moved to Melbourne as she had been accepted into the conservatory of music. Moses reluctantly agreed and Marjorie happily moved to Melbourne, where she obtained her midwifery qualification. Bill was a frequent visitor.

The courtship went very well away from Moses' disapproval as they were a well-suited couple. And eventually Moses gave his reluctant permission for the couple to be engaged and finally let Bill on the property.

Grandpa McInnes was a tall, strapping man and had a deep love for VFL football. He would proudly proclaim that he had nearly been drafted to play football for Carlton when he was a young man.

When Mum and her sisters were young girls, he loved nothing better than to take them to the QEO football oval in Bendigo to watch a local football match on a Saturday. He often commented that it would take him a while to make his way around the football ground as he always got lots of favourable comments about his pretty daughters, especially the blonde-haired, blue-eyed identical twin daughters.

Grandma McInnes was a most capable and practical women as was evident by her clever engineering of pursuing a career and courtship both at the same time. A beautiful cook, dressmaker and gardener, she was a supportive presence in her four daughters' lives.

It was during this particular visit that the topic of politics came up. Mum proudly told them that she and Rex had decided to vote Labor in the federal election as she thought Gough Whitlam delivered wonderful speeches. There was complete silence for a few moments and Grandma McInnes went quite pale. My usually composed grandparents then started behaving most oddly. There was a lot of yelling. Grandma McInnes was nearly crying and kept yelling, 'We will be overrun by communists. We will be invaded by the communists.' Grandpa McInnes, who was a little quieter but had gone quite red in the face, kept muttering, 'Reds under the beds. Reds under the beds.' I was wondering who was under his bed, and who was red.

'Iris, how could you? He is a communist and we will be invaded by the communists. He calls people comrade, and his wife doesn't wear gloves,' shrieked Grandma McInnes. 'No one in this family has ever voted Labor,' sobbed Grandma McInnes. We were all sitting open mouthed at the table. This had been the most exciting visit ever and surprisingly, our usually very quiet Mum stuck to her guns and said, 'No, it's time for a change. That actually was the election slogan. He is not a communist; he makes wonderful speeches and I don't care about the wife's gloves.' The next Sunday visit was more restrained and, to my disappointment, the adults all decided that they would not discuss politics ever again.

8

Ladies, a plate please?

April 1972

I was very tired that month at school. A new show on telly had debuted, called *Number 96*. There were lots of stories written about it and pictures of really pretty ladies. One in particular, called Abigail, was always in the paper. The adults in my world were all talking about it in hushed tones, but I would snatch snippets of the conversations every now and then. 'It's a show about poofters, and fancy that, Abigail was topless, and that other couple is living together and they are not even married.' Grandma Howarth was most irate about it. 'Just filth,' she would say to whomever was in earshot on any given day. I thought it was odd that Grandma seemed to know an awful lot about this TV show even though she vowed and declared she would never watch anything so depraved. *Mmm*, I thought. Sounds interesting, but I wasn't really sure what a poofter was. But I did spend many an evening where I would sneak out of bed and hide behind the lounge room door watching *Number 96* while Mum and Dad were in the kitchen, which was situated on the other end of the house. I decided I preferred watching another TV show, *Homicide,* so my energies were better spent sneaking out of bed when *Homicide* was showing on the telly.

The school was the social hub of the community as there was no local hall. Between and after the two world wars, the school was used as the venue for dances, parties and concerts, which kept the community connected. By the 1960s, the school was not used for dances anymore, so Mum and Dad used to drive us over the mount (Mount Alexander) eight miles from Faraday to Sutton Grange Hall to attend the Saturday night old-time dance. McQueen's old-time band would be playing. The adults would be dancing the *Pride of Erin*, *Evening Three Step* and barn dancing, to name a few, on the newly polished floorboards. There was strictly no alcohol, but I did notice a lot of the men used to go outside rather a lot for brief intervals and would always return in very high spirits with flushed cheeks and talking very loudly. Dad was not one of those men ducking outside. Probably with a wife and four daughters, and young men's shoes to stare at, there was simply no time.

Dad would tell us we had to look at all the young men's feet. 'You can always tell the calibre of a man by his black, polished shoes' was one of Dad's favourite sayings. Unfortunately for us and Dad, it was the era where sneakers were coming into fashion and it was very hard to spot any young man in black, polished shoes. Dad would often lament that there was 'a lot of no-hopers around these days, wearing those bloody sneakers.'

My favourite part of the evening was when they would break for supper. The trestle tables would all be moved into the hall, and tables would be overflowing with all the homecooked goodies the ladies had brought. Sandwiches (with white bread of course), ginger fluffs, cream sponges, cream puffs, and homemade biscuits. No one would dare to bring anything that was not homemade. People would be milling around the tables, chatting, laughing, and enjoying their cups of tea—or in our case, a glass of water—and Dad would usually be glaring at all the young men wearing sneakers.

9

A most evil plan is hatched

Melbourne, May 1972

Two men, Robert Clyde Boland from Bendigo, and Edwin John Eastwood from Melbourne, met for the first time in the May of 1972 at a five-day plaster training course in Melbourne.

Both were disgruntled with their lives. Eastwood was already embarking on a life of crime. Boland, unhappy with his life and unable to measure up to his father's expectations, had started dreaming up easy ways to make a lot of money that did not involve plastering. They had greed on their minds and grandiose ideas. It was a lethal mix and the start of a partnership that would bring grief and despair to those they came in contact with.

Boland was older. He was in his thirties and was the probable ringleader. He had already formulated a plan to make a quick million dollars. A kidnapping. But as yet he had not found the right accomplice. However, after attending the plastering course, he had found one who was as greedy as he was and who was also quite gullible.

In the weeks after this course, Eastwood started driving back and forward regularly on the Calder Highway from Melbourne to Bendigo. He would meet in Bendigo with Boland to discuss their plan, with the objective to net a quick one million dollars by kidnapping school children and a teacher. The armed robberies Eastwood had been carrying out in Melbourne were not doing so well, but this caper would set him up for life. He was only twenty-one years old and he was already a young father.

Boland, a father of four, in his mid-thirties, did not have any previous criminal convictions but simply wanted an easier life. He possessed a moral compass that was badly skewed.

They started going on regular road trips together to find the perfect target. They would check out small rural schools in Victoria. They had taken a drive over to Horsham but did not find any schools suitable and were weighing up Ravenswood State School just out of Bendigo as a definite possibility. But they were concerned that it was too close to the highway. They needed something isolated, set off from the road, with no one about. It was our misfortune one particular day in June 1972 when Eastwood was driving up to see Boland in Bendigo. He must have glanced over to his left after driving for a couple of hours from Melbourne. It was hard to spot from the Calder Highway, and he would have nearly missed it. It was set off from the road and was well concealed by a large cypress tree in the corner. It was an old, blue stone building, and you could just make out the name—Faraday 797.

The target had been found and it was perfect.

10
Shopping days in Castlemaine

May 1972

Life on our farm was always busy. Four small girls kept Mum very busy running the family home, and Dad and his brother, Joe, worked the physical life of a mixed farm. This included a small dairy, an orchard, cropping, and sheep. Thursday was a very exciting day of the week as we always went shopping to Castlemaine. Grandma would walk across the paddock suitably attired in her best outfit with matching hat, gloves and sensible shoes. She would arrive to be driven into town by Mum as Grandma didn't drive, as was the custom of her age. Us four girls all crowded into the back seat. Mum would drive very sedately and slowly over the ten miles into Castlemaine and carefully park in the main street. Not like Auntie June though! Dad's younger sister—the matchmaker of my parents, a friend to all and sundry, my godmother, and a very enthusiastic driver, who never obeyed the road rules.

Auntie June knew everyone in Castlemaine and everyone knew her. She would be seen driving around in her blue Zephyr sedan, waving and tooting the horn most enthusiastically at everyone as she sailed through the stop signs to park in the centre road parking in Mostyn

Street. She would then chase us down to share all the family news for that week, with our cousins, Annette and Wendy, in tow. Shopping in Castlemaine on a Thursday was not for one who was in a hurry.

It was our favourite part of our shopping trip. Spotting Auntie June, we would have our eyes peeled and one of us would grab Mum's arm and yell, 'There's Auntie June, and she has just driven really fast through the stop sign again.' Mum would usually make a funny face when we told her about the stop sign. Auntie June would then spot us and start madly beeping the horn, wind the window down and yell out, 'Yoo hoo! Yoo hoo!' Auntie June had great exuberance. Ladies were always well dressed, often with hat, matching glove and bags. Especially Grandma. Friends and relatives of all age groups would stop for a chat in the main street as they went about their weekly shop.

The Howarths were creatures of habit. We parked in Mostyn Street and as such, we always banked at the Castlemaine ANZ bank, where Dad had a particular fondness for a Miss Pearson. She had an amazing beehive hairstyle, very typical of the sixties, she was unmarried and worked full time in the bank. Dad liked us to all go into the bank and stare at this poor woman. This was because he had got it into his head that this was a career we should all aspire to and it would be our, and his, crowning glory if one of us could score a job at the Castlemaine ANZ bank as a bank teller and work alongside Miss Pearson. Miss Pearson always looked a little puzzled as Mum would be busy filling out forms for the banking and the four of us would dutifully stand and stare at her for the duration of the bank visit.

Shopping trips always took the same format: ANZ bank staring at Miss Pearson, and then Slingo's Grocers situated at the top of Barker Street for all of our groceries, all neatly packed in brown paper bags and with the most delicious aromas coming from the shelves behind the wooden counter. We would then go to Ewing's, the butcher situated in Mostyn Street, for our meat, with the heavy sawdust on the floor intermingled with animal blood. We were regular customers at the butcher's as Dad could never bring himself to slaughter his own livestock. And finally, a visit to Penrose Liquor Store in Templeton Street, a quiet back street where Mum would buy Dad a bottle of sherry and a packet of Havelock, ready-rubbed tobacco. If, and only *if,* she had any money left over. It was a time of routine with a sense of belonging and family.

As we spent so much of our time on the farm, our pets were an important part of our lives. Sally, our pet sheep, was particularly memorable. Sally was a cantankerous Border Leicester. We were really frightened of her and didn't like her at all. Sally loved nothing better than to chase us and if she was really lucky and got close enough, she was very adept at giving us an almighty head butt. Her one redeeming feature was that she was a large sheep with a thick, fine fleece. She loved to hang around our house, always on the lookout for a stray child to chase.

Thursday had arrived, and it was our usual shopping day. Sally was, as usual, nearby, awaiting an opportunity to chase us. We all piled into the Kingswood with Grandma in the front seat. Sally was in the middle of the dirt driveway, refusing to move, as usual. Mum had not seen her and kept backing out when all of a sudden, there was a large bang. *Crash*. Sally was now stuck under the car and the back of the car was airborne. This caused quite a commotion and we all clamoured out of the car with Mum yelling for one of us to run and get Dad. There was cantankerous Sally stuck under the car with neither Sally nor the car able to move. Dad and Joe both arrived red faced and puffing with Dad exclaiming, 'Bloody hell, Iris. How could you run over the bloody sheep?' With much grumbling and swearing, he jacked the car up, and Sally blithely trotted off to the paddock as if nothing had happened. For a brief time in our lives, we were indeed riding on the sheep's back. Sally was fine. Dad was cranky. Mum was embarrassed. And we all laughed and laughed. This was turning out to be a most enjoyable day to go shopping!

11
Freezing Faraday, frozen pipes and cold feet

June 1972

Winter in Faraday was freezing. We were always running late for school as getting out of a warm bed was horrible. The lino on the bedroom floor was so cold and we would run quickly over it into the bathroom to find the pipes frozen with no water to have a wash. We would all crowd around the open fire in the kitchen, eating our toast very slowly while Mum was busy making our lunches and trying to hurry us all up.

Winter was also lambing season and we could not leave the farm, but most of the ewes had no trouble lambing. We would always get very excited in lambing season when Dad occasionally brought home an orphan lamb to bottle feed. Although, Mum used to end up doing most of the feeds once the initial attraction had worn off.

This was a very bad winter. Dad was very upset. He had been to check the sheep in the paddocks on the other side of the Calder Highway and found a massacre had occurred. Baby lambs had been mauled to death. The ewes were in the process of dying, their intestines ripped out, bleating pitifully. He came home sad faced, loaded the shotgun and went back to put the ewes out of their misery.

'Bloody dogs,' he muttered. He waited and watched the next night, in the paddock, and was alarmed to see the dogs in question making their way towards the sheep. Three prized German Shepherd dogs belonging to a neighbour. Dad had his shotgun with him and fired off some shots, which caused the dogs to take off in panic. Dad came home, very subdued, and said to Mum, 'Well, I suppose I better go and get it over and done with.' He hopped in the ute and drove to the neighbour's place, where the three German Shepherds enthusiastically greeted him. The owner came out. The dogs belonged to his three daughters. They talked, both men very upset. The daughters came out and started to cry, begging for a reprieve for their loved dogs. Dad offered to put the dogs down, and asked if there was somewhere else the dogs could go, but the owner said, 'No, there is nowhere else.' And he would do it. The universal law of the bush is that once a dog starts killing sheep, it won't stop and so, it has to be put down or moved from the area. Dad was very quiet that night.

A few weeks later, another rule of the bush was broken when shifting stock across main roads. Signs would be put in place either side of the road by the farmer, indicating to drivers to slow down or stop, and mostly that is what they did. Dad would often move sheep from paddock to paddock and sometimes they would have to cross the Calder Highway, usually with no mishap. This particular winter's day though, a truck driver either didn't see the signs or didn't care, and he drove through the mob of sheep just as they were crossing the road. Most of them were killed and those that did survive were too injured to live. Dad came home to get the gun again, white faced and covered in sheep's blood, to shoot the injured sheep. 'Bastard didn't even stop,' he muttered to himself. This was turning into a shocking winter for stock and income losses.

12

Enid Blyton and Hair

July 1972

I had been diligently practising my times tables at home and found that I was quite good at the times table races, my favourite activity at school. You would take one step forward each time you gave the correct answer to the times table question posed. The first to the end of the school room was the winner. It was a hotly contested race and sometimes I would win. I had also been trying really hard with my writing. My handwriting was not the neatest, and I was really trying my best to graduate to a pen licence.

That winter I also discovered the delights of books and loved reading Enid Blyton's *The Magic Faraway Tree*. I spent a lot of time on a weekend curled up in a chair with books as Dad had decided none of us were to help on the farm as we had to prepare ourselves for our future careers with the ANZ bank in Castlemaine. Jill generally ignored this directive on weekends as she loved nothing more than just pottering around the farm and looking after the various animals.

ENID BLYTON AND HAIR

We had all been wondering at school what the Christmas concert this year would be like. The annual Christmas Tree Concert in December was a highlight. The whole community would be invited and all would attend. The school would be full and the grand finale was a visit from Santa Claus. Last year's concert had been particularly good. The young, male teacher of the previous year had a particular fondness for the musical, *Hair*. He decided that we should all perform musical numbers from this show, such as 'Good Morning Star Shine', 'Aquarius' and 'Hair'. We sang loud and proud and had dance moves as well. The audience proclaimed it was the best concert ever and were very taken with the songs from *Hair*.

Over supper, following the performance at the school, there were lots of questions directed at the teacher about this musical, *Hair* and where it was playing in Melbourne. 'If only Melbourne was not such a long way away. We would have quite enjoyed going to see this new musical, *Hair*', was frequently commented to the teacher, who was starting to look a little uncomfortable. Dad got quite enthused about this show and we kept nagging for a few weeks after the concert about going to see *Hair*. We could see Dad was actually thinking about it. The thought of driving to Melbourne to see a live show would be so amazing and for us, something we had never done.

Dad did look into it and came home and said to Mum, in an incredulous voice, 'Well, Iris. I'll be buggered. That show, *Hair*, that the kids sang all the songs from at the concert, the actors all perform in the nude. They get up on stage without a stick of clothing on.' I piped up and said, 'So, can we still go? I'd really like to see that. 'No. We bloody well are not going. Iris, can you believe that? In the nude?' muttered Dad. 'That's what happens when you get these city types up here with all their newfangled ideas.'

13

Bessie, the favourite cow

August 1972

School holidays again, and again we could not leave the farm. We often used to ask if we could go away for a holiday, but the answer was always no. 'Your father cannot leave the farm.' Dad and Joe ran a small dairy, milking two jersey cows at a time, attached to a simple milking machine. The milk would be pumped into the milk vat. Dad was very particular about milking his cows and it took him an awful long time, both morning and night. Approximately two hours in the morning and two hours in the evening, but as he always said, he was the only one who could milk the cows as he understood them and knew how to talk to them. He seemed to really like talking to his favourite cow, who apparently was a great milk producer. Her name was Bessie.

Joe, the younger, perennially bachelor brother, could not be left in charge of the cows as it was too big a responsibility for him. He might lose his temper and yell at the cows. It was very important that the cows were not upset so they kept producing milk. Mum would often sigh and have a funny look on her face when Dad was giving us this talk about why we couldn't go away for a holiday, or for a weekend, or a day trip, as he simply couldn't leave the cows. Every night Dad would bring a billy home filled with cow's milk with cream on top, which Mum would skim off. We always looked at the billy with a distaste as we all really, really hated cow's milk.

Mum would be often found at the wood heap chopping wood for the two open fires and wood fire stove. My job would be to collect sticks and kindling to light the fires with. Winters in Faraday were freezing and hard work.

14
Evil was circling

September 1972
Back at school again for Term 3 and lots to look forward to. The annual school sports were coming up in October, where we would compete against the other small schools in the region, and the Castlemaine Agricultural Show—the absolute pinnacle of our year. Jill was acting a little oddly though. Each day after school she kept talking about a man and asking funny questions. 'Did you see that man? The one with the binoculars. He sits near the creek most days. Do you think he is looking for birds?'

My mind was full of plans for the school sports and Castlemaine Show, so I didn't really take much notice of her questions and would airily fob her off. 'I guess he must be looking at the birds,' I would reply dismissively. Jill would add thoughtfully, 'But he doesn't have the binoculars pointing at the trees where the birds are. He has them pointing at us.' I did not know at that time but Jill was right. We were indeed being watched, counted and hunted.

The two men with their binoculars had set themselves up regularly near the creek running adjacent to the school on the Bendigo side. They would watch us playing in our rustic school grounds, making daisy chains, playing hide-and-seek and daydreaming of futures we could not yet imagine. They must have thought how easy this was going to be. No one was about and no one came and asked them what they were doing, but apparently their plan was to say they were birdwatchers in the unlikely case that they were challenged. They knew our movements, how many of us there were and if the school had any visitors. They had already noted that Mrs Doyle came to the school every lunchtime with Tracey's lunch, so they would not be paying us a visit during lunchtime.

These men were watching and realising that we were a school of mainly little girls and one very young female teacher. How perfect for them, and how dreadful for us.

As a school group, we were practising very hard for the sports, spending a lot of time in the school grounds. I always hoped that one day we would win the aggregate trophy. Every year, we looked forward to the Castlemaine School Sports in October, at the camp reserve in Castlemaine. We would compete against other small schools in the region. We would practise hard and we loved participating in the tunnel ball, which I always hoped we would win. But alas, this had not happened thus far. We also competed in sack races, and egg and spoon races, along with the more traditional track and field events, which we always tried really hard in, and were usually competitive. We were all quite tribal and would march under our school banner at the start of the day. We would view the other schools with a degree of wariness, trying to work out who our main competitors would be.

I could run fast and would spend September practising in the paddock at home, running as fast as I could. I had been chosen to be this year's sports captain, so I was extra keen for Faraday to bring home the aggregate trophy.

15

So much to look forward to

October 1972

October was finally here. My favourite month of the whole year. It was my birthday and I would be turning eleven. Then there were the school sports, and our absolute favourite outing for the whole year—the Castlemaine Agricultural Show. We so looked forward to this day every year.

Dad had recently been promoted to head sheep steward at the Castlemaine Agricultural Show, and he was pretty chuffed about this, so of course we were as well. There was lots of talk around the kitchen table as Dad had been a sheep steward for many years but as he had now attained the position of head sheep steward, this meant much more responsibility.

Dad was making plans for the day. He would have to be there very early to pen the sheep, meet with the judges and organise the other sheep stewards to make sure the day ran smoothly. Dad himself had a Border Leicester stud, which he sometimes entered at other local shows, not Sally though due to bad behaviour. We were very excited as in other years, we would arrive with

Mum early afternoon, wearing our best dresses. We loved checking out the sheep in their pens to see which sheep had the most ribbons. Then we would head off to the cattle pavilion to do the same before checking out the dog show. Then, finding a seat around the show ground, we would watch the horses, who were so beautifully groomed and in sync with their riders taking them around the show jumps. It was all so amazing we did not know what to look at first.

Finally, we made a careful perusal of the arts, crafts and cookery pavilion, admiring the many cakes, scones, slices, and bountiful produce from local gardens on display.

There was lots of sights and sounds for young girls to admire, the scent of freshly cut hay for the livestock and clip-clopping of horses as they made their way to the arena. There was loud music and squeals of delight from enthusiastic patrons enjoying the rides from the carnival side of the show.

Dad always said to keep away from the carnival crowd as they were all criminals and had probably just got out of jail. He knew this because many of them had tattoos, so of course we thought that as well and generally did keep away from that part of the show.

There always seemed to be lots of people milling around admiring the livestock, wandering through the cooking and craft pavilions, and catching up with friends, neighbours and relatives. They were all up for a chat as they enjoyed the day. If we were really lucky, we got a ride on the merry-go-round, some fairy floss and a show bag. At the end of the day, our feet would be sore, our best dresses filthy, and our show bags empty. And if I am really honest, tummies would be squirmy from the fairy floss, which was a once-a-year treat.

That night, Dad would tell us about all the exciting things that had happened to him that day. And his highlight would be having lunch in a special pavilion with the other stewards and judges—and he didn't even have to pay for it!

16

The calm before the storm

Friday 6 October 1972

I had no inkling that this was the day that would change my life. It started as just a normal day.

I didn't want to get out of bed that morning. It was cold. Mum had put out our clothes on the end of our beds—warm jumpers and slacks. I immediately decided that I wanted to wear my summer dress and cardigan with long white socks, which I got out of the wardrobe and put on. Mum just shook her head at me when I entered the kitchen. 'You will be cold,' she said. Jill and Denise followed soon after dressed in their warm jumper and slacks. We didn't wear uniforms.

We all crowded around the open fire, which Mum had lit, trying to warm our hands. We had breakfast of cornflakes and toast. We ate breakfast slowly, so we could listen to the radio. Mum was busily making our lunches, which consisted of white bread sandwiches, a biscuit and a piece of fruit. Mum told us to hurry up as we would be late. Dad had left to milk the cows. All of us piled in the car, so glad it was Friday. There would be time over the weekend to practise for the school sports, and my favourite football team in the whole wide world, Richmond, was playing against Carlton in the VFL Grand Final. I was determined to listen to the game on the radio in the kitchen the following day. Richmond was going in as favourites as they had played a very exciting finals series consisting of a drawer against Carlton in the semi-final, and then in the second semi-final replay, they won by forty-one points. My favourite player was the captain, Royce Hart, who played half forward and could jump really high and mark the football. I thought we had a really good chance to win the grand final.

There was only six of us at school that day. Leanne, Tracey, Terry, and Richard were all away with bad colds. It continued to be a cold miserable day, which was unusual for October, and halfway through the morning I was shivering in my summer dress and wished I had listened to Mum. The morning dragged and, because our numbers were so small, we couldn't play the times tables race. We spent our time practising our writing and did some quiet reading. At lunchtime, we went outside, ate our lunches in the shelter shed, and started to play chasey. It was not much fun as it started to drizzle with rain and we were getting damp and cold so we stopped and made our way back to the school building.

1.20 pm

Miss Gibbs must have taken pity on us as we all came in bedraggled and cold from being outside and she decided that PE for that day would be conducted inside and we would play musical chairs.

What better way to spend a Friday afternoon? We loved musical chairs and all of us enthusiastically dived for the chairs when the music stopped, laughing and squealing when we were just a tad too slow to reach that elusive chair, which Miss Gibbs diligently removed after each musical round. The game was so much fun, and we were soon out of breath and getting warmer by the minute.

The bare floorboards of the school room were slippery and provided a perfect base to slide, grab and sit down quickly on the remaining chairs, at the same time trying not to knock over the smaller kids. It wasn't always with success.

1.30 pm
I didn't hear anything, but something had changed in the room. I started to shiver and noticed that a blast of cold air had engulfed the room.

My gaze went to the door. It was open and, in the doorway were two men. Something felt very wrong.

They stood starting at us and not speaking. They filled the whole doorway. We were meeting for the first time – Robert Clyde Boland and Edwin John Eastwood. Although at this stage we did not know their names.

I tied to concentrate really hard, screwing my eyes up and staring at them. I knew it was rude to stare, but I was trying to work out what was so very strange about these two men. And why were they not speaking?

My mouth went really dry, I was having trouble swallowing and all of a sudden, I had butterflies in my tummy. They were going crazy. *How odd*, I thought to myself. *We rarely have visitors at Faraday State School, especially not on a Friday afternoon. I wonder if they are friends of Miss Gibbs that had dropped in for a surprise visit.* But they didn't look particularly friendly and why didn't they say hello? We all stopped playing musical chairs and simply stood still in the middle of the classroom, unsure what to do.

I looked over to Miss Gibbs. She had a confused look on her face and her hands were shaking as she switched off the cassette recorder. The room was silent. The taller man (Eastwood) took a step into the room. His clothes were dark and he had a woollen mask over his face. I would learn later that it was a balaclava. The only part of his face visible were his eyes, which were darting all around the room.

The shorter man (Boland) followed him in. He was carrying a brown school bag, which looked heavy. He had bright red hair, a tartan sun hat pulled down tight over a mass of red curls, and he was wearing sunglasses. I stared even harder as I had never seen anyone wear sunglasses inside. What a strange thing to do! Perhaps they were playing a practical joke or were in special dress ups. The dress ups were not very good and were scary. I thought to myself, *they wouldn't win a prize for their costumes.* The taller man (Eastwood) had a gun; it was a really big gun. I hadn't noticed it at first as he was holding it by his side when he walked into the room, but now he had lifted it up, finger on the trigger, and was aiming it at us. I would learn later it was fully loaded.

We were all still standing rooted to the spot in the middle of the classroom. Miss Gibbs called out, her voice sounding wobbly, 'Please, not us. Please, not us.' We looked towards her and saw that she looked very scared and she too was staring straight at the big gun. Edwin John Eastwood, with fully loaded gun, complete with balaclava, finally speaks and we all jump. In a loud, booming voice, he announced, 'School's over for the day!'

My mind was in a muddle and nothing was making any sense. How could that be? That man was telling lies, school could not be over. It was not 3.30 pm, it was only 1.30 pm and we never had the afternoon off. The bell hadn't rung and Mum wasn't there to take us home. That man was going to be in so much trouble telling lies and waving and pointing that gun around in such a crazy manner.

I am going to tell Dad as soon as I get home. He will be so wild. Dad had a shotgun that he kept on the porch at home, always unloaded, with the bullets kept high above the kitchen mantelpiece. We were never allowed to touch the gun as Dad would always say, 'Guns are not playthings and you must never touch it.' *That man's dad must have never told him that. Guns are not playthings and he shouldn't be waving it around. Someone could get hurt.*

He turned to our teacher, Miss Gibbs, pointing the gun at her, and in a very bossy voice, he said, 'Tell them to sit at the tables.' Miss Gibbs quietly said to us, 'Go and sit at your desks.' Her voice still sounded a bit wobbly. We all quickly did as she asked, glancing at each other and worriedly looking at the two men, who seemed to have taken over our classroom and stopped us playing musician chairs.

The butterflies in my tummy were still there and getting a lot worse, and I started to panic a bit. I couldn't understand what was happening. Confusion, fear and that gun, that really big gun, no one has ever pointed a gun at me before. He said school was over. Was he going to shoot us? Would it hurt if he shot us? Would we be dead?

'Go and get into the van now …,' growled the masked man (Eastwood) '… and no one better be heroes.' *What van?* I think. *A van? What is happening?* We looked over to Miss Gibbs, who seemed to be having trouble standing up and had gripped her desk really tightly. She was leaning against it. We were so busy staring at the gun that we had not noticed the man with the sunglasses on inside (Boland) had made his way over to our teacher and was standing really close to her. Eastwood continued to wave the gun at us and gestured to the doorway with it. We looked over to Miss Gibbs, hoping for a miracle. She slowly nodded her head and we had no choice but to obey. We all shakily got to our feet and moved towards the school door. I didn't want to leave the safety of the school. I didn't want to get in a van. I didn't want to go outside, especially with that man (Eastwood) with the gun. I thought he was a bit crazy. Maybe once we were outside, one of us could run really fast and hide. He waved the gun at us again, made us stand really close together and herded us out like a flock of sheep.

When we got through the school doorway and outside, we saw a small, red van parked at the school gate. The lettering on the side of the van said, 'When delivering breads, be careful.' I thought to myself, *I must remember this, it could be important.*

I plucked up the courage and said to this man, 'You are not going to murder us, are you? Robbery would be okay but not murder.' He didn't answer. He just stared at me as though I was invisible, and then I almost kicked myself. What a dumb thing to say. We had nothing he could steal.

He then said in a show-off voice, 'We have nothing to gain by killing you, but then again nothing to lose either.' And he started to laugh. My mind went blank for a few seconds, trying to make sense of this. My hands became sweaty and I decided I really didn't like Eastwood.

This was beyond my understanding. *What does it mean to be murdered?* I ponder this. *I hope I would go to heaven, might see Lassie up there. I have been pretty good most of the time, saying my prayers each night, but the other day I did have a big fight with Jill and rubbed chewing gum in her hair, so that would definitely go against me.*

I wasn't ready to die. I had not yet lived. I was only ten years old and I had a life I so wanted to live. A life I could not yet imagine. A world I wanted to explore as my world had been so very small, so very predictable and so very safe.

17

Kidnapped

Friday 6 October 1972
We clambered into the back of the van and looked around for somewhere to sit. There were no seats, but Jill, Denise and I sat on one side on the wheel coverings facing the other girls, Christine, Linda and Helen. The man with the gun slammed the van door shut and disappeared. None of us spoke. We were too scared.

We simply stared at each other. All our eyes were as big as saucers and I took in this surreal scene. Helen was sitting opposite me wearing a short, tartan skirt and hand-knitted warm jumper with long white socks. Next to her was her sister, Linda, in knee-high white socks, laced sturdy shoes, a pleated, short skirt, and another warm hand-knitted jumper. Completing the trio was Christine, not quite as warmly dressed, wearing a white cardigan and to-the-knee blue dress, with her blonde hair tied back in a ponytail. Helen, Linda and Christine were all huddled together. On my side, Denise was next to me. She was shaking, wearing a pink, knitted jumper, which had seen better days, and warm slacks, white socks and brown school shoes. On her other side was Jill, looking completely lost, wearing a blue hand-knitted jumper, warm trousers that were far too short for her, showcasing a large portion of white socks with brown shoes. And then there was me, with scuffed shoes, socks falling down, thin summer pink dress, and thin pink cardigan. I was dressed for a spring school day, not a kidnapping!

Jill whispered to me, 'I think those men are the bird watchers.' My heart sank and I kicked myself. If only I had listened to what my little sister had been telling me over the past few weeks, and maybe if I had told Dad, he could have chased the bird watchers away. But it was too late now. A few minutes later, the door at the back of the van opened and Miss Gibbs climbed in, looking a little pale. She gingerly made her way to the front of the van, on the passenger side, where she sat on a yellow petrol container.

She was wearing amazing high heeled, knee-high brown boots. I had overheard the mums at the school gate school talking about the boots to each other, about how smart they always looked and how much they might cost. I think deep down they all would have liked a pair. Miss Gibbs was wearing a mini skirt that she was trying to pull down as she was taking her seat. She wore a white jumper and matching crocheted bolero, far too smart an outfit for the back of a smelly van.

As Miss Gibbs was climbing into the back of the van, Boland, who was carrying the bag and still had sunglasses on even though there was no sun, poked his head in and called out, 'You need to be careful. If you push him too far, he could be dangerous.' The butterflies in my tummy worsened and for a brief moment I thought I was going to be sick. In the next instance, Eastwood climbed in, still waving the gun around, face completely covered in a funny woollen mask with only his eyes visible. He was now carrying the brown bag that the other man had carried into the school room. It still looked heavy.

We all leaned as far away as we could from him. I was really happy when he made his way to the front of the van and sat down next to Miss Gibbs. I saw Miss Gibbs making a funny face and leaning as far as possible away from him.

Boland must have made his way to the front cab section because all of a sudden, the van started up and lurched forward. We were momentarily thrown against each other. He pulled out of the school driveway and turned right onto the Calder Highway. All in all, it had taken ten to fifteen minutes to kidnap a complete school.

The van was going fast and the road was bumpy. We were being jostled and found ourselves being bounced up and down on the wheel coverings. There were small holes drilled in the van sides, so we all started peering out of the holes trying to see where we were going. It was very uncomfortable. We were still not speaking, just looking at each other, puzzled and scared. Our bottoms were getting very sore.

Eastwood, the kidnapper, started talking to us in quite a loud voice. We jumped in shock. He was unable to keep his hands still and was continually waving them around. He started opening the brown bag and pulled out chains and a knife. When he was not fiddling with the chains, he was touching the gun. Dad would be so wild about the gun. We knew that was not how you should handle a gun. Someone could get shot and with the ride in the back of the van so bumpy with us all being bounced up and down, including the kidnapper, it could be one of us.

I tried not to stare as I didn't want to make him angry, but why did he have a a bag filled with chains, a knife and padlocks? None of this made sense. 'Hey, you kids, how would you like to be in the papers?' No one answered. We just looked worriedly at each other, too scared to answer him. I thought to myself, *Why would we be in the papers? We are not famous or rich. He is one strange man.* 'Hey kids! No. It's going to be grouse. You are going to be in all the papers. I am going to make you famous. And that shit hole you come from, what's its name again?' Miss Gibbs replied quietly, 'Faraday.' Christine then asked in a quiet, timid voice, 'Do you mean the *Castlemaine Mail*? (our local paper)?' The kidnapper roared with laughter at this response. 'Yeah, and maybe a few others as well.'

Possibly because no one was joining in on his one-sided conversation, or maybe at some level he recognised that we were all really scared of him, he removed his balaclava. He simply pulled it off, stuffed it in the bag, shook his head, and ruffled his hair. He seemed happy to have it gone. It helped a little to see his face. He was not an old man; he looked about the same age as Miss Gibbs, but his eyes looked crazy and his hands never stopped moving.

'Hey kids,' he called out in a loud, raucous voice, 'What do you want for Christmas?' We all jumped in fright and looked at each other hoping someone would answer. Christine was very brave and in a quiet, trembling voice she said she would like a Chrissy doll. Jill then piped up and said she would like a new puppy.

Linda said she would like a kitten. The man looked really bored and in a loud voice, said, 'Yeah. Whatever.' I thought to myself, *You didn't really want to know. And stop talking to us.* We all started very zealously peering out the holes in the side of the van, making absolutely sure we did not look at Eastwood in the hope he would stop talking to us.

It was getting more and more uncomfortable in the van. The wheel coverings were really hard on our bottoms and we kept getting thrown around even more as the van kept hitting potholes. There was nothing for us to hold on to. We seemed to be heading towards Melbourne and, peering through the holes, I noticed we had driven through Elphinstone, Taradale and Malmsbury. No one was going to notice us in the back of this van. My heart started to beat very fast and my hands became sweaty again.

The kidnapper then turned to Miss Gibbs and started talking just to her. I breathed a huge sigh of relief as he seemed to have lost interest in us. 'Where are you from?' he asked. She gave a one-word answer, 'Finley.'

'Oh yeah,' the kidnapper replied. 'I know it.' In a loud, boastful voice, he announced proudly to us all, 'We are members of the Utasha movement, and have been up your way at a training camp on the Murray River. You know you don't have to be a foreigner to join. It's a pretty special sort of group, and they don't just let anyone in it. They told me I would be pretty handy.' We all looked really blankly at him, having no idea what he was talking about. Even Miss Gibbs appeared non-plussed. (As an adult I learned that Utasha was a Croatian terrorist group that did have training camps in Australia in the early seventies. But there was never any evidence that the kidnappers had any involvement with this group.)

All of a sudden, the kidnapper said in a loud voice to no one in particular, 'I am going to ring the *Herald Sun* and let them know what we have done. The paper will then contact the maggot cops and it will be on.' We all looked at each other in puzzlement. *Why would the Herald Sun be interested in us? I think he must have escaped from a mental hospital, and it's not nice to call the police maggots.*

He then turned to Miss Gibbs and said, 'Have you got a driver's licence on ya?'

'Me?' she replied in a puzzled tone, 'Yes, and why do you want to know that?' He said it was in case anyone didn't believe they actually had us; he could show the licence as proof of identification. Miss Gibbs slowly and reluctantly handed over her licence. Then, he asked Miss Gibbs if she had any money. She said, 'Nine dollars.' He then held out his hand and said, 'Can I borrow that?' Miss Gibbs slowly got her purse out and reluctantly gave him the money. He took the notes and put them in his jean pocket.

He laughingly said, 'I will pay you back later.' But he never did. *He is a thief*, I think, my mind racing in alarm. *He has just stolen nine dollars from our teacher!* He then picked up his transistor and asks us all how we like his *new* transistor. It was nice. It had a silver plate over the front, with holes in it. It was black and silver and looked brand new. 'It's hot, you know?' he said and started laughing as if it was a huge joke. We all just stared at the wireless and at him in horror. We had never met a thief before.

18

The long drive to who knows where

Miss Gibbs looked quite annoyed and took her purse back, quickly zipped it up, placed in her bag, and put the bag as far away as possible from the man. I would learn later that she had another $26.00 in a compartment in her purse that he had missed seeing and she saw no reason to enlighten him. Miss Gibbs had brought a tape recorder along and started to play some music. It made it harder to hear the conversations between the two adults, which I think was the purpose. But if we listened hard, we could still follow some of the conversations, but luckily not all.

Eastwood just kept talking and talking like he was trying to impress her. He looked at her driver's licence with a Bendigo address on it. 'Ahh. You're from Bendigo. Would you like a couple of thousand in the mail in a couple of months' time?'

'No, thanks,' she replied in an incredulous tone. 'I get enough as a teacher and I do not want to get any money that way.'

Miss Gibbs took a big breath and leaned closer to the man and asked, 'What are you planning on doing with us once we reach our destination?' He lowered his voice and whispered to Miss Gibbs, who then started to cry.

I would later learn that he told Miss Gibbs, 'We have found this grouse spot in the bush and … well, I have dug a big pit fourteen feet by fifteen feet, and we are going to put you all in the pit with your mouths taped shut with sticking plaster. But it is a bit dodgy and is collapsing in places as it has been raining, so it might not be safe. So, you might not go in there. We'll see.' Miss Gibbs was still sobbing silently when the kidnapper grabbed her arm, pointed at us and shook his head. He said, 'Think of them. Don't get upset.'

Helen, who was only in Grade 1 and six years of age, was sitting closest to the teacher and kidnapper. She was picking up on the teacher's angst and could probably hear some of the conversation. She was nearly in tears. Miss Gibbs beckoned her over and sat her on her knee. They both drew some momentary comfort from each other. Miss Gibbs then asked in a wavering voice, 'Why did you pick our school? There are hundreds of other schools.'

He replied, 'I was thinking of Ravenswood, but it was too close to the highway, and your school could not be seen from the highway. You know we have been planning this for a while. I was over Horsham way, but couldn't find any good places to hide anyone, as it's not very bushy over there. I couldn't believe my luck when I found this school. And we've spent a lot of time nearby, just watching and waiting,' he said, making a funny face at Miss Gibbs. I think to myself, *Jill was half right, as she had seen them with binoculars in the creek adjacent our school boundary several times over the past few weeks, but it wasn't birds they were watching, it was us.* It made me feel sick that someone had been watching us play in our school grounds.

'We would have been at the school this morning to take you, but I was at the drive-in last night and slept in. By the way, did that lady come today, the one that always brings lunch for her kid?' he asked. Miss Gibbs replied, 'No. Her little girl was sick.' He then says in an aggrieved tone, 'Oh, we could have come earlier then. And not waited until after lunch.' Mrs Doyle always brought lunch each day for Tracey, but as she was sick that day, there was no need.

As the van continued its bumpy journey, the kidnapper was silent for a few moments and then started staring intently at the floorboards. 'Do you think you could get out of here?' Miss Gibbs looked very tired and replied wearily, 'We would not have a chance.' He continued staring at the floorboards. 'Do you think you could lift the floorboards?' Miss Gibbs, in an exasperated tone, said, 'No. I couldn't lift them because they are all screwed in tightly.'

'Mmm.' The kidnapper remained silent, still staring, fixated at the floorboards. 'You know, I think you could get out through the floorboards.' Miss Gibbs shook her head and said, 'We would not have a hope of getting out of this van.'

We passed Kyneton. We were all still diligently peering out of the small holes, more for something to do, and this way we didn't have to look at the kidnapper. Poor Miss Gibbs had really drawn the short straw as he really seemed to want to talk to her a lot and kept leaning in towards her and waving his arms around so as to make a point. It was like he was showing off for her. Miss Gibbs sat very still and didn't look like she was enjoying the talk at all. We were getting really cold, and our bottoms were becoming numb. Jill, Denise and I started to hold hands. The human contact kept our hands warm. It felt like we were driving for hours. The van was quite dusty and our hands were getting dirty if we touched the side of it or our makeshift seats. It also had a funny smell—a musty, petrol smell.

Sometime later, we turned left on a dirt road and the potholes got a lot worse. We were driving away from the main highway and we were really getting thrown around as the road was so bumpy. Miss Gibbs looked through a peep hole and said out loud, 'There is a sign to Lancefield, but we didn't turn off there.' *Lancefield, I thought to myself, That is such a long way from home. How will we ever find our way back home?*

We just kept going deeper into bushland on a rough dirt track surrounded by dense shrubs and trees. How will anyone know where to look for us? Eastwood called out to the driver (Boland), 'Hey, Sam, are you on the right track? Do you know where you are going?' Boland just grunted in reply.

19

Deep in the bush

Miss Gibbs, I think, was getting sick of Eastwood showing off and said to him in a cross voice, 'How could you do it? Take six innocent children who have never done anything to you or anyone. You're nothing but an animal.' Eastwood started to laugh, but it was not a happy laugh. 'Funny you should mention that. My wife calls me an animal too. She said that just before she cleared off with my own kid.' The van stopped and we peered out and spied a gate. Eastwood and Boland both got out and stood together, talking next to the gate.

We couldn't hear what they were saying. It was just unclear murmurs, but we all sat really quietly, trying to pick up on a word that may give us a clue as to what was going to happen next. Boland opened the door and ordered us all to move over to the driver's side and face straight ahead. Christine, Linda, Helen, and Miss Gibbs all moved over to our side and we all crowded together. It was very squashy but we did what he asked. Boland, still in the open doorway of the van, turned to Eastwood, who was momentarily out of sight, and said, 'I will keep the gun.' The van door slammed shut.

We all sat very uncomfortable in stunned silence, and then we heard the sound of a car engine starting. I peeked. There was a car hidden in the paddock. It was white with a blue or maroon stripe down the side of it. Eastwood was in the car and revving it up. He was driving off. *Oh good, he is leaving. We will not have to listen to him talk all the time, but the other man still has the gun. That is not good. I am glad he has driven away. He was a scary, crazy man who seemed to think we were all going to be in the papers, which was so very odd.*

Boland got in the front cab and started the van. He drove a short distance, then did a lot of reversing and driving back and forward. We could hear him swearing in the front part of the van as we were being thrown about in the back.

Finally, the van stopped and all was quiet. We all just sat there really quietly, still not sure what to do. Too scared to talk. Too scared to move. Denise whispered to me, 'I have to do a wee' and I suddenly realised I had to go too. Miss Gibbs, realising that we were all in need of a toilet, banged on the van wall and called out, 'Please, we need to get out and use a toilet.' Boland did not reply but we heard him open his driver's door, walk around to the back of the van and slowly open the van door. Eventually, he let us out of the van. By then, we all desperately needed to have a wee. We all slowly climbed out of the van and looked around. It was freezing cold. We were in a small clearing. The sky was grey and overcast and it was starting to rain. I had never seen this place and I didn't like it.

We were surrounded by lots of trees and scrubby bushes intermingled with large rocks. We scampered off in different directions to find trees to squat behind. We all jumped in fright as Boland started bellowing at us, 'Do not go too far.' We didn't. He then called out to us in a strange voice, 'If any of you try to be heroes, it will result in immediate death.' None of us were thinking of escaping. Where would we run to? Deep in the bush, with no idea where we were, a dark overcast sky, and a man who had a gun, a knife and a bag of chains.

I looked over from behind my tree and watched him for a few moments, puzzled as to why he would want to kill us. Why did he want to hurt us, we were just little kids? He was leaning against the driver's side of the red van talking to Miss Gibbs, holding a knife in one hand and a chain in the other. There was something odd about his hands. As I kept staring, I realised he had plastic bags on his hands. I would learn later that Miss Gibbs used that time to study Boland very closely and was able to give a detailed description, including what type of watch he was wearing, his clothing, which included blue jeans, yellow shirt, blue jumper, brown shoes, dark sunglasses, and a pulled down tartan hat over his bright red, curly hair. I thought he looked most odd with that funny hat as there was still no sun. He kept showing Miss Gibbs his knife and, in his hand, he had a chain. Miss Gibbs looked like she didn't want to see either the knife or the chain.

I could see Miss Gibbs was trying to move away from him. Her face had gone white and her hands were shaking. I was so glad that at the time I didn't know this, but Miss Gibbs asked him, 'What would you do if the police came?' His answer was, 'I'd shoot one of the kids.' Miss Gibbs then asked, 'What would that achieve?' He replied, 'They would realise there was five left and you.' Later, Miss Gibbs asked the same question and this time he said he would not shoot the children but would shoot her instead.

I was very happy that Eastwood had gone somewhere in the car. He had been so annoying, talking all the time and waving the gun around. Boland seemed quieter, calmer even. *He might not hurt us*, I thought to myself, *at least he is not waving the gun around.*

As I write this today, I can now recognise that we had actually been left with the more dangerous and sinister of the two. And I am in awe of Miss Gibbs's bravery and that she was able to maintain her composure while being terrorised and threatened. She would have known that Eastwood, while very annoying, was full of bravado and was dangerous, but Boland was cold, calculating and full of menace.

I am not sure what would have happened if Miss Gibbs had not been able to maintain her composure and had collapsed in a screaming heap. I think we would have panicked, possibly tried to run off, and the outcome could have been dire.

But we didn't panic, we cooperated and did our best to not draw any attention to ourselves.

After relieving ourselves, we all gathered around near the van and looked around. The bush was thick and dense, the sky grey and overcast, it had started to rain, we were getting wet, and it was so cold.

We did appear to be in some sort of clearing surrounded by tall gum trees. I couldn't work out which way was home and even if I did know where home was, I couldn't leave my sisters.

20

Mum's story

Friday 6 October 1972 - Faraday State School - 3.30 pm

Three cars pulled up outside the primary school as usual and parked in their usual spots. The three mothers were Iris Howarth, our mother; Thelma Conn, Linda and Helen's mother; and Sylvia Ellery, Christine's mother. It was a typical Friday afternoon. They all knew each other well and enjoyed a warm friendship. They got out of their cars and chatted for a few minutes. All three families were long standing residents of Faraday and their farms had been in their respective families for generations. 'It's odd the children are not out on time,' Sylvia commented. Mary is always very punctual.'

They chatted for a few minutes longer before deciding that one of them needed to go into the school room and hurry them along. Thelma Conn offered to go in and see what the delay was as none of the children were ever kept in with detention. She came out a short while later looking very puzzled. The school was empty—eerily empty. She told the other mothers there was no one there, but that all the kids' bags were still hanging on the hooks.

Starting to feel quite alarmed, they began investigating. Perhaps they had gone for a nature walk in the pine plantation opposite the school and lost track of time, or someone had fallen and hurt themselves. This was the days of no mobile phones. The mothers walked across the road with two toddlers in tow—Suzanne, the youngest in our family; and Adele, the youngest of the Conn girls. They searched the pine plantation. It soon became obvious that there was no one there. They came back to the school, really puzzled. They decided to spread out with each woman taking a section of the school grounds and start searching. They called out but there was no reply.

Mum and Suzanne walked down to the Calder Highway and scanned the road in both directions, but there was only the occasional car driving by. For all three women, a feeling of utter dread was building.

Sylvia Ellery took charge. She decided to go back into the school, and said to Mum and Thelma, 'I am going to go into the school and have a really good look and check Mary's desk. Maybe she has left a note with their whereabouts.' Sylvia, an ex-teacher herself, approaches Mary's desk, not wanting to tamper with any of her papers and books that were neatly stacked. She has a good look. All seemed to be as normal and everything was in its place. No note.

She then checked the school phone and realised it was dead. She stood there for a moment and tried to think what to do next before searching through the children's desks. It was nearly the last desk she came to … and then she found it. She pulled out a large piece of white paper with newspaper letters pasted on to spell out a message.

Her hands start to shake as she stares at the note in disbelief. It is a ransom note. The note read:

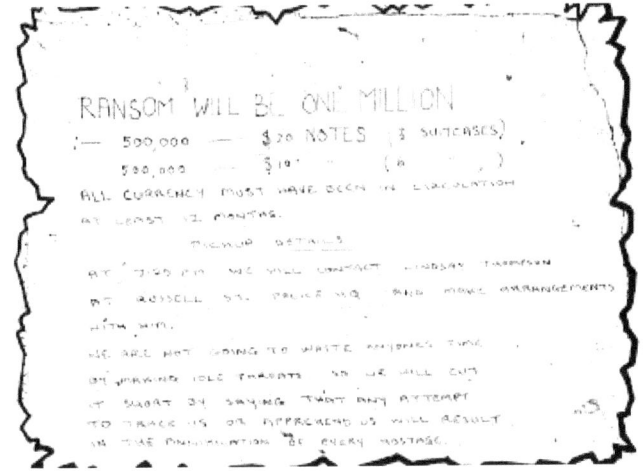

Mum said she could see something was terribly wrong when Sylvia came out of the school holding a large piece of paper. When she reached them, both her hands were shaking and she looked as if she was going to faint. She showed the other two mothers the ransom note, and the word *annihilation* echoed in a silent, obscene scream inside our mother's mind—and I'm sure in the minds of the other two mothers as well. It took them a few moments to register the enormity of the crime that had been committed against their children. The three women stood and stared at each other for a moment, ashen faced, and just not knowing what they should do. There was no phone they could use as the school phone was dead. Thelma Conn was the first to react. She jumped into her car and quickly drove over to the closest neighbouring house situated half a mile along the Calder Highway,

Melbourne side. The house was that of Mr Harden, the local water bailiff. She ran in and asked to use the phone before calling Castlemaine Police Station.

The three mothers then returned home to their farms, without their children, to find their husbands and try explain the unexplainable.

21

Consternation

Mum drove back to the farm with my youngest sister, Suzanne—a pre-schooler—in tow. She tried to find Dad, who was not at home but out working in the paddock somewhere. Mum then ran over to Grandma's house and went into the farmhouse kitchen calling out, 'I need to find Rex. Where is he? I need to find Rex. Please tell me where he is.' By this stage, Mum was incoherent and hysterical. 'They have been kidnapped. They have been kidnapped,' she kept repeating.

Grandma was very confused and at a loss trying to understand what was going on. Her usually quiet daughter-in-law was sobbing in her kitchen, one grandchild at her side, but no sign of the other three. And kidnapped. 'Who has been kidnapped? Surely not the girls.'

Grandma eventually grasps what's going on and says to Mum, in true, stoic Grandma Howarth style, 'Well, crying about it is not going to bring them back.' Grandma was never one to show any emotion as life had delivered her some significant challenges, which she had endured. She was widowed one Christmas Eve as a young woman with six children, and she had a farm to run. Grandma would have been very upset but after years of showing a stiff upper lip to the world, she was not able to show Mum the compassion she needed at that time, nor did she really understand the events that were unfolding. No one at that time could understand the events of that night.

22

The plan unravels

Maybe this is close to the truth because in my mind this is how I believe that night played out for Eastwood. But of course I was not there. I was locked in the back of a van shivering.

Eastwood drove carefully to Melbourne, not wanting to draw any attention to himself. The balaclava was hidden, and the weapons were left with Boland, who was guarding us—the hostages. It had gone pretty well really. Mentally, he went over the plans in his head and braced himself for the next step. He did feel a pang of conscience as those kids did look really scared, especially when the gun was pointed at them, but it was too late for those thoughts now. He parked near the phone box on Elizabeth Street and quickly hurried to phone box booth 448, glancing around to make sure no one was watching him. He put the first call through to the *Herald Sun* and spoke to a journo by the name of Wayne Grant. Eastwood made sure he got the message loud and clear. He was quite chuffed that the journo bloke seemed genuinely shocked over the phone and was fumbling to get a pen so he could write down his every word.

THE PLAN UNRAVELS

Now for the next step. He had his plan and had gone over it several times with Clyde (Boland). He was pretty pleased with this plan as watching the *Dirty Harry* movie at the drive-in the other week had really helped him put it together. He had chosen the man who would collect the ransom and ultimately deliver it to them. He had all the notes already written out and would go to the pre-selected phone boxes, leaving them pinned under shelves. They were directions instructing the person he had chosen, who would be collecting the ransom to follow, using a Morgan Street directory. He would then leave the street directory at the tally-ho boy's home, near the front gate. It was all set. He would call the man in charge, Father Oakley, later. He was the one—the anointed one they had chosen to be the one to collect the ransom. His thinking was that a man of God—a priest—would not screw them over. This would keep him busy until 7.30 pm when it would get really interesting when he phoned Thompson (the minister of education).

I suspect that Eastwood may have spent some time at the tally ho boy's home as it was a home for the homeless and/or delinquent boys in the fifties and sixties. It fits with his age range and he was very keen that Father Oakley was to be the contact.

7.32 pm: Eastwood phones D24 and asks for 'Thompson'.

'Which department?' the telephonist asks. He hangs up. 'Oh shit! They should have been expecting the call. The bastards must have put a trace on it.' *Okay*, he thinks. *All is not lost. I will call Father Oakley from tally-ho. He can then call Thompson, organise the ransom, and I will tell him which phone box to start at.* He takes a deep breath as he is starting to feel rattled. He puts the call through to tally-ho boy's home. A cheery voice on the other end of the phone tells him that Father Oakley is on holiday and is currently unavailable. He slams down the phone and pounds his fists on the ledge of the phone box. He paces up and down the footpath trying to calm down. 'This is going to shit. Everything is going wrong.'

23

The story hits the press

Wayne Grant, the crime reporter for the *Herald Sun*, is the one who took the infamous call from Eastwood.

He was one of the few journalists who was really kind to us in the aftermath and he seemed genuinely concerned for our future wellbeing.

For some years after the kidnapping, Wayne would occasionally pop into the farm just to say hi. Dad would be very chuffed and would insist on taking him mushrooming. Wayne would be dressed in a very nice suit with smart city shoes. Not really the attire to explore a farm.

He would kindly participate, climbing through fences, dodging cow pats and walking through wet grass, but I did notice him wiping his shoes on the grass with an odd look on his face. I'm pretty sure Dad enjoyed these outings, hunting for elusive mushrooms, way more than Wayne did.

Wayne's story
Friday 6 October 1972 (the eve of the VFL Grand Final)

It was about 4.40 pm and Wayne was sitting at his desk in the press rooms at Russell Street Police Headquarters. He had not long finished speaking to Laure Oaks, the chief of the *Herald Sun,* Canberra, about a Yugoslav terrorist suspect and was about to slip out for a beer at Ron Stout's pub on the corner.

He didn't know at the time but at the top of Elizabeth Street, just over a mile away, the kidnapper stood in a grey telephone booth—no. 448.

He picked up the receiver, dialled the number and dropped a five-cent piece into the slot. He was calling the *Herald Sun.*

Down in the *Herald Sun's* Flinders Street office, Mrs Audrey Brooks, the chief of staff's secretary, picked up the extension 1232.

'Do you want to hear about a kidnapping?' a male voice asked.

'Could you hold the line for a moment? I will put you through to a reporter.'

'You had better be quick about it.' And she was.

Wayne's phone rang.

'I'll say this only once,' a voice said. 'Have you a pen and paper?'

The voice was demanding. *Another one of those half-stung news tipsters, or more likely one of the boys from the pub having a stir,* Wayne thought. It needled him a bit.

'Hang on, I'm not in that big of a hurry. I haven't got my pen yet.' 'Well, smarten yourself up. I don't want this call traced. Hurry up!'

Then, 'I've kidnapped the pupils and teacher from Faraday State School.'

'Faraday? Never heard of it. Where's that?' Wayne asked.

'About seventy miles north of Melbourne.'

'The ransom is one million dollars. The details are in a note in one of the front desks.'

He was initially sceptical but got a map of Victoria out and located Faraday on the map. *It wasn't even a town*, he thought. *It is probably a crank call but better notify D24.*

But then again, if this is true, it will be a huge story. I might just give that beer a miss.

24

Police investigation in Melbourne

The Castlemaine Police immediately dispatched a car to Faraday, contacted D24 and started setting up roadblocks. On the first floor of the police headquarters in Melbourne, Mr Sinclair Imrie ('Mick' Miller), the force's forty-seven-year-old assistant commissioner in charge of operations, was busy with the never-ending police paperwork. His grey phone rang. It was Inspector Jock McCulloch from D24.

'Sir, you're not going to believe this, but we have a kidnapping. Six children and their teacher.'

'What?' Miller asked in an incredulous tone. 'Are you serious?'

'I told you weren't going to believe this. This is what we have, sir.'

McCullough read out the message from Castlemaine Police Station. It would be the first of hundreds that would flow through the force's nerve centre in the next three days.

It read:

1640 hours from Castlemaine. We have received a message from Mr A Harden, who lives near Faraday State

School, that he has not seen any children near the school . . . parents are waiting for their children ... there are no signs of the teacher and children.

'We have also received a call from Wayne Grant of *The Sun*. He received a call from a man with a youngish male voice, about twenty years old, that he has kidnapped the teacher and the children and has left a note in a desk at the school.'

'We have checked the school, and the parents are in attendance, but there are no children.'

The note, in fact, was found in a desk. It is a ransom note that reads:

RANSOM WILL BE ONE MILLION
500,000 - $20 Notes (3 suitcases)
500,000 - $10 Notes (6 suitcases)
All currency must have been in circulation at least 12 months.

<u>*Pick up details*</u>

At 7.25 pm we will contact Lindsay Thompson at Russell Street Police HQ and make arrangements with him.

We are not going to waste anyone's time by making idle threats, so we will cut it short by saying that any attempt to trace us or apprehend us will result in the annihilation of every hostage.

Miller was initially stunned and then quickly organised his thoughts and acted promptly to get the best team assembled. He immediately tried to contact Mr Bill Crowley, the crime commissioner, but he had finished for the day and could not be found straight away.

Mr Miller then pulled in some top men fast—his right-hand man and trouble shooter, Frank Holland (head of CIB); Chief Superintendent Bill Woods, and the deputy CIB boss, Chief Superintendent Mick Patterson. Luckily, all three were having a drink together at the police club on McKenzie Street. They were ordered to the disaster room in D24 and briefed.

Next on Miller's list was the premier, Dick Hamer. He was able to track him down as he was officially opening the New Associated Securities Ltd building on Victoria Street less than three hundred metres from police headquarters. A crime squad car was dispatched to pick him up. Lindsay Thompson, the education minister, was at home. He was phoned and asked to be on standby.

25
Faraday and Castlemaine

Search Headquarters - 6.00 pm. The logistics.
The police set up search headquarters at Faraday Primary School. An army of searchers had begun to gather, including two hundred police, two hundred St John Ambulance volunteers, a trail bike group, and community members. Neighbours, friends and relatives were arriving to help. The news was starting to filter though the local community and all arrived looking concerned and visibly upset.

Chief Superintendent Frank Holland and Detective Chief Inspector Frederick Warnock were in charge at the school search headquarters, and police units from Daylesford, Castlemaine, Maldon, Seymour, Kyneton, and Bendigo were all in attendance. Due to the nature of the case—six little girls and a young female teacher—Senior Constable Janet Lowe of Ballarat, who was in charge of a squad of policewomen, was seconded.

Under the command of the police, the neighbours and local residents all fanned out and started a search of the immediate vicinity. The local organisations were all contacted, which included Red Cross, Castlemaine Hospital, Alexander Home and Hospital for the Aged, and local St John Ambulance brigades, who set up refreshments at the school and proceeded to organise accommodation in the drill hall in Castlemaine for the searchers, who continued to arrive.

Shortly after the search had commenced, the local fire brigade units swung into action. This included Metcalfe, Maldon, Bendigo, and Castlemaine. All had the communication units open on their radios to assist with communications. Station Officer Jack Chapman manned the radio at regional headquarters and coordinated their communications.

The local council was contacted, and staff made available for the provision of barricades and traffic supervision. The Castlemaine Badminton Club made the drill hall available and arranged extra facilities for heating and cooking for the expected influx of visitors.

Meanwhile, the police were quietly investigating the families of the victims, trying to ascertain if there were unsavoury links or a possible motive as to why this school had been targeted. It would become very apparent that the families were exactly what they appeared to be—farming families with no criminal links or history.

They were unable to locate Miss Gibbs's fiancé at the time, Neil Noelker, which initially caused some interest. But he made contact at 10.00 pm that evening after hearing a news bulletin. He had been out visiting friends and was soon ruled out as a suspect.

It was getting colder, and concern for the teacher and children was growing by the minute.

26

The community rallies

The news started to spread like wildfire as more and more people gathered to search. But it would be an impossible search as no one had any idea where to start.

None of the families involved were wealthy so as news of the kidnapping spread, with a ransom of one million dollars, it was obvious to anyone who knew the families, that we would never have any way of raising such an amount. The community had made the assumption that the kidnappers had demanded the ransom from the families.

Meanwhile, my parents were under police guard, when offers of financial assistance began trickling in. A Harcourt orchardist, Mr Brian Kidman, a father to young girls himself and known to be successful and wealthy— by Howarth standards—visited Dad with tears in his eyes and asked Dad how much he needed to get his girls back. He went on to explain he had contacted his bank and they were waiting for him to go there that evening and withdraw money to help pay the ransom. There were whip arounds in the local pubs and inns, where a hat was passed around and money contributed for the ransom.

That night, the searchers spread out and searched and searched. Local farmers all searched their own properties, looking through abandoned sheds and tramping through paddocks with torches, hoping to find traces of missing children. But at the same time, they were terrified they would find murdered children.

There was a heightened sense of fear in the community, and the searchers were frightened and anxious as a madman was surely on the loose and they could be attacked at any time. But still they kept searching. That night, no children were allowed outside to play. Houses were all checked with windows and doors locked securely. Children were sent to bed early while adults sat and listened to the news bulletins on the radio with increasing dread.

It was getting colder.

27

The longest evening

Bushland at dusk

He let us out of the van again. It had stopped raining, but the ground was wet underfoot. We were in a small clearing, surrounded by tall gumtrees and dense bushes. We looked around, shivering and cold, and no one really said much. Denise sidled up to me and whispered, 'I would like to go home now.' I thought to myself, *So would I*, and I had no words to comfort her. I looked over to Jill, who was white faced and absently kicking wet leaves lying on the ground. I was getting really cold in my summer dress and wished I had listened to Mum that morning and put on warmer clothes. Miss Gibbs suggested we have a treasure hunt so we started running around, picking up the odd leaf, twig and stick, relieved that we had something to do.

It was the most miserable treasure hunt of my life. It was drizzling with rain, freezing cold, and the bushes seemed to be closing in on us. We were starting to get hungry and thirsty as we had had had nothing to eat or drink since lunch time.

There was no sound—no birds chirping, no sounds of any cars or people nearby. The dense bush surrounding us seemed alien. It was a place we did not know. The trees, the low bushes, the rocks, and the rough terrain were not our friends. We were alone with him.

He stood really still just near the van, watching us. He was always watching us with his dead eyes. He had finally taken off his sunglasses and, holding the rifle, he would occasionally yell at us to get back if we moved too far away from the van. He didn't look like he was enjoying himself—and we most certainly were not. Miss Gibbs was standing near him and kept glancing over at him nervously, and then towards us. I began to feel like a rabbit being hunted—like I could be shot at any time. It was not a good feeling. I wondered if I should try and stand behind a tree, pretending to look for treasure, then if he started shooting, I might have a chance. But then, any time anyone of us headed towards the trees, he yelled, 'Get back over here!' And we did. It was almost a relief when Boland called out to us that it was time to get back into the van, and he locked us in again. At least we did not have to look at him with his gun and knife. And those eyes. They were blank, like those of a dead fish with no feeling.

D24 Police HQ Melbourne – 7.00 pm
The building was rapidly filling up with key police. The switchboard operators were alerted about the 7.25 pm call due to come in from the kidnappers. The PMG technicians arrived to hook up call tracing equipment. Everyone was on edge. Ten minutes before the deadline, Mr Miller and Mr Thompson had a short chat about how to approach the phone call because how Mr Thompson handled the call would be crucial.

7.28 pm: The premier, Mr Hamer arrived and said, 'What have we got here?'

Mr Miller said, 'On one hand we have the lives of a young teacher and six small girls. On the other hand, we have a ransom for one million dollars. You have got to tell us which it is going to be—one million dollars or seven lives.'

To Mr Hamer's great credit, he did not hesitate and said, '$1 million. Can you get it?'

Mr Miller said, 'We can try.'

At 7.32 pm, a red light flashed on the switchboard. The operator answered and said, 'Police headquarters.'

'Where's Thompson?'

'Which department do you want?'

'Forget it,' he said and hung up. They would all learn later that it was the kidnapper.

Then, more confusion when three minutes later someone rang claiming to be from the Castlemaine Police and asked for Mr Thompson's home phone number and address. They were told Mr Thompson was at D24 and the caller rang off. A quick check with the Castlemaine Police showed that no one had called from there.

What had just happened? This was making no sense—two calls asking for Mr Thompson, who was there waiting to speak to the perpetrator. The craziness of it all was making the police very nervous and worried for the teacher and young girls.

8.00 pm: It was a stalemate, and a sense of powerlessness washed over everyone. The police and Mr Thomson called a brief meeting to renew tactics. A decision was made to source money for the ransom in case a call did come through. Later that night, a large amount of money was borrowed from an airline company. A satchel fitted with tracing devices that belonged to the police, was prepared just in case.

Search Headquarters – Faraday Primary School – 7.00 pm

More and more people arrived, the search was widened and there were hundreds of people searching. People driving by on the Calder Highway, many on their way for a weekend away, heard the radio bulletins and started to pull over and join in on the search. The police in charge were pouring over maps, organising and coordinating groups of searchers through their radios. A fire was lit in the school grounds to keep people warm. The searchers spread out and searched, but it was a hopeless search with no leads to go on and no idea where to search. It was getting very disheartening for everyone.

The police radios were keeping in regular contact with the Search Headquarters at Faraday Primary School with updates about neighbouring areas searched such as Harcourt, Elphinstone, Taradale, and Barkers Creek. All of a sudden, all the police radios, in unison, started broadcasting loud music and all police communication and messages were blocked.

Chief Superintendent Frank Holland and Chief Inspector Frederick Warnock were extremely worried and frantically tried to make contact with all the crews. They were certain that the kidnappers had done this and had the ability to disable their communications. They were also very concerned that someone involved in the kidnapping was watching the search being conducted and knew exactly when to make the communication system crash to cause maximum chaos.

As the Country Fire Authority radio channels were still working, CFA officer Jack Chapman offered the police the use of their communication system and the messages were sent out to all crews: 'Tune into the CFA channel urgently.'

Communications were open again, but the police communications would remain down for many days.

The two policemen in charge breathed a sigh of relief again and could again begin to coordinate the fruitless search.

Kit Chapman, Jack's wife and stalwart to the local CFA, stepped in to man the CFA radio communications. She did so for the next three days, day and night.

She did not sleep for three days and nights and made sure the channels were open and transmitting around the clock.

28
Lone Pine Farm – 8.00 pm

Grandma Howarth sat by the open fire in the kitchen, ashen faced, watching the flames. Usually, the open fire would not be lit in October, but it was a cold night. She pulled her cardigan closer. Relatives were arriving—cousins, aunts and uncles. The kitchen was filled with people, mainly women and children. The men were out searching. Auntie June was in the corner, crying quietly. My cousins, Annette and Wendy, would tell me later that they were really scared, but they weren't sure what they were scared about.

The police were present, keeping watch over the family. Two young constables were visibly shaken by witnessing the grief and fear in the kitchen. They kept leaving the kitchen to go outside and get some fresh air. They appeared relieved when my cousin, Val, and her husband, Ray, arrived from Melbourne and Ray took pity on them and kept them company outside in their vigil, away from crying women.

Mum was heavily sedated and barely coherent. She once told me that that night she kept walking into our bedrooms, staring at the three empty beds all neatly made. No children complaining about going to bed, no school clothes messily strewn around the bedrooms, just cold, silent bedrooms.

The sedation was the only thing stopping her sinking to her knees and emitting a scream that would never end. She was living every mother's worst nightmare.

The infamous Sally and me

Shopping day with Grandma

The Four Howarth Girls

October 1972

Minister and Police with school group

Going home

Denise safe with Mum

Family reunited

Van at Lancefield

Van at Lancefield

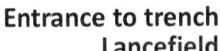

Entrance to trench Lancefield

Inside the trench at Lancefield

Sports Day 1972

Faraday the old dairy on the farm 2024

Faraday our property today - so beautiful 2024

29
D24 Melbourne - Police Headquarters

The coldest night
The story had broken to the press earlier. Bulletins were being flashed on the radio and television. The police had initially wanted to keep the story under wraps, but now that it had broken, information started coming in. Up until this stage, the police had very little to go on, and had been concentrating very heavily on the backgrounds of Miss Gibbs, her family and friends, and the families of the six little girls. D24 was very busy, with the phones being manned and information received being sifted through.

At 11.45 pm, a call comes in with the first possible clue. A woman claimed to have seen a tomato-coloured van parked outside the school at 1.30 pm that day. Forty-six minutes later, the police learn that a parcel was to be delivered to the school. The education department had scheduled a delivery at approximately that time in a red PMG van. Which was it? The first clue or a red herring? It would be late the next day before police would learn the truth.

As the night lengthened, police were still situated at D24. Planning, worrying and thinking through the order of the night, as they had very little to go on.

3.00 am: A phone call is put through. A male, Australian voice barks, 'Woodend Post Office. 5.00 am. And no funny business. Tell Thompson to bring the money.'

It was on! The atmosphere in the room changed in that instant. Assistant Commissioner Mick Miller immediately phoned Bill Crowley, the crime commissioner. 'It should take you no more than twenty minutes to get here. See you in fifteen,' Miller said.

3.30 am: A tough decision was to be made. Who should go to Woodend with the deputy premier, Mr Thompson? The military tactic that the generals should not lead their troops into battle, applied here. Miller and Cowley mulled it over and decided that they would both go, turning the military tactic on its head. They reasoned that a public figure such as Mr Thompson should be afforded the protection of two of the best senior cops, and both men had the authority and the expertise to make crucial, on-the-spot decisions should the situation arise. Mr Crowley, dressed in a hound's tooth sports jacket and peaked cap, would pose as Mr Thompson's chauffeur. Mr Miller, who was in uniform, would ride in the back.

At 4.05 am, the vehicle left Police Headquarters. Both officers had pistols. Lying on the back seat was a high-powered rifle. On the front seat between Mr Thompson and Mr Crowley, was a large brown satchel. The forty-three-mile trip was tense, with each man caught up in his own thoughts.

At 4.46 am, another police car approached Woodend from Faraday. In the car was Chief

Superintendent Frank Holland and Inspector Dick Knight. Both had been up all night supervising the search from Faraday Primary School.

Time 4.51 am. The ransom car was one minute away. Mr Crowley had requested a time check. Mr Miller notified D24 that he was turning off radio transmission. A moment later, a call was received by Malcolm Elder, a *Sun* reporter on duty at the police headquarters press rooms. 'I rang at 3.05 am,' a male voice said. 'I could kill those kids. It was a hoax. I was on my way to Woodend, but it could have cost six kids their lives. The real bloke could have knocked them off. I could have got a million bucks, but I thought of the kids. I know Thompson is on his way there. You can call it off; it is a hoax. I will leave it with you.'

D24 was urgently trying to make contact with the ransom car to provide a new update, but the occupants remained unaware as the radio transmission had been turned off.

The ransom car made its way slowly into town. Mr Miller lay down on the back seat and covered himself with a rug, pistol securely gripped in his right hand. The car slowly drove up High Street and along to the post office. The car stopped twenty feet from the lit entrance, where the 3.00 am caller had demanded that Thompson stand. It was dead on 5.00 am. Mr Thompson, dressed in a heavy dark overcoat, got out, satchel gripped. He stood alone, very still, resolutely staring ahead. He waited. Meanwhile, several other police cars were hidden on the outskirts of Woodend. Mr Miller was uncomfortable and stuffy under the blanket and could not see. It was potentially a highly dangerous situation. The deputy premier was standing outside the car, alone, clutching the brown satchel. He was a very clear target. In his mind, there four very real possibilities:

1. The kidnapper could shoot Thompson and grab the money.
2. The kidnapper could drag Thompson away and use him as a hostage.
3. The kidnapper could demand the money and promise the whereabouts of the hostages would be divulged at a later time, once he was safely away.
4. The two policemen could wound or shoot dead the pick-up man, putting the safety of the hostages at risk.

No possibility was very appealing.

Just before 5.30 am, a dirty old Holden ute appeared and drove up High Street, past Woodend Post Office and turned right. Less than a minute later, it returned, turned and pulled into a lane alongside the post office. The driver, a young man, appeared within minutes and walked casually up to Mr Thompson and started speaking. They exchanged greetings. Mr Thompson remarked, 'You're out a bit early.' The young man replied, I am looking for a mate' and kept walking. A couple of minutes later, Chief Superintendent Holland and Inspector Knight, drove into the town and contacted the ransom car.

They had heard the D24 message that the 3.00 am call was probably a hoax. The occupants in the ransom car still had not heard this as their transmission remained switched off. Crowley gave the order for the two policemen to grab the young man as he was walking away from them. They did. But the young man in question was twenty-two-year-old James Weston, a timber worker, going home to his flat five doors down from the post office after a big night out.

Initially, the police were very suspicious of Mr Weston as it seemed too much of a coincidence that he would appear at that exact time and place. But upon interrogating him, it became obvious that he was three sheets to the wind, unsteady on his feet, and needing to sleep it off. He was lucky he was not sleeping it off with a bullet lodged inside.

The deputy premier and two senior police were disheartened and felt they had just missed out on an opportunity to apprehend. They were also concerned that the kidnappers themselves were running a surveillance and would be aware that Mr Thompson did not come alone.

5.40 am: Mr Crowley, Mr Miller and Mr Thompson left Woodend, their thoughts being that even if the call was genuine, there was now no chance of anyone turning up. I learned later that Mr Miller always believed that the call was genuine and that the kidnappers lost their nerve in turning up. In that area, that night, there were army manoeuvres occurring, which were nothing to do with the case. Mr Miller suspected that this was what had frightened the kidnappers off. They drove to Faraday to discuss the situation and supervise the ground search plans for the day.

Night-time in the bush
It was getting colder and darker in the back of the van. We all huddled together for warmth, but it was no good.

We were freezing. Miss Gibbs called out to the man in the front cab that we were all getting very cold in the back of the van. He let us get out and we all climbed into the front cab with him. No one wanted to sit near him and we were all leaning as far as we could towards the passenger door. Denise, the tiniest, had to sit on his knee. She looked towards me in horror, but it was the only way we could all fit in the cab. We all huddled together, the smaller children sitting on the bigger children and Miss Gibbs's knees. Jill was sitting on my knee, and I found her to be quite heavy. My knees were hurting, so I kept pinching her bottom, hoping she would move. I felt bad that I was pinching her bottom, but I just wanted my knees to stop hurting. Understandably, she was getting frustrated and had nowhere to move anyway, which then resulted in a sister tiff. Miss Gibbs immediately told us to stop squabbling and sit up properly, which we did.

Boland, the older kidnapper, still had plastic bags on his hands. And out of the blue he said, 'You know, I really love kids.' We all stared at him in stunned amazement and I thought to myself, *So, if you love kids so much, why did you come and take us away? He must be as crazy as that other one!*

He turned on the transistor and we heard a deep-voiced male radio announcer stating:

We have breaking news. There has been a kidnapping at a tiny hamlet called Faraday. Six students and their female teacher have been taken hostage. There are grave fears for their safety. The last kidnapping in Australia was that of Graeme Thorne, whose parents had won the lottery, but tragically the little boy was murdered within twenty-four hours of being snatched.

Boland quickly changed channels, but we heard another deep male voice saying:

We are interrupting this program to bring you breaking news. There has been a kidnapping at a small farming area named Faraday. A female teacher and six children are being held hostage. The last kidnapping in Australia was that of Graeme Thorne, who was murdered shortly after being taken.

Each breaking news interruption gave more details about the little boy's murder. The kidnapper started getting twitchy and continually channel surfed, playing with the transistor dials and muttering, 'I will find some music to listen to.' But every channel had the same story, The Faraday Kidnapping, and the fear that the outcome would be the same as the kidnapping of Graeme Thorne. He eventually turned off the transistor. He then turned to us and said it was terrible what happened to Graeme Thorne. No one answered. There *was* no answer. We all just stared bleakly out the front window into the dark night. I thought to myself, *That poor boy. He was murdered. The radio is saying the same thing could happen to us, that we will be murdered. Oh no. Why us? I just want to go home.* I started praying and bargaining with God. *Please, God, don't let them murder us. I will be good, not fight with my sisters, get out of bed earlier in the morning, and not complain when it is my turn to collect the kindling for the wood fires at home.*

It was getting very late. We had never stayed up this late and it was really cold. We sat in silence in the front cab of a van in the middle of dense bush with this very strange man, who had a gun and said he loves kids. It was dark and my feet had gone numb. We were all shivering. We all perked up and started trying to look towards the window. We heard a car. Perhaps it was someone coming to rescue us.

D24 MELBOURNE - POLICE HEADQUARTERS

The kidnapper, Boland, didn't react. A small glimmer of hope was soon extinguished and our hearts sank as Eastwood appeared and opened the cabin door. Although, he did not seem as cocky as when he first drove off. He had brought cold fish and chips. The first food we had had in hours, since lunch time. We ate them, but they were awful. The transistor was turned on again. We listened to the news broadcast. It said that the premier, Mr Hamer, was keeping in contact with what was going on. Boland said, 'Good! It is turning political.' Boland climbed out of the cab and he and Eastwood started murmuring together. We desperately tried to eavesdrop to learn what they had in store for us. I heard Eastwood say that he tried to get in touch with someone called Lindsay, but they were trying to trace the call so he hung up. He then said, 'We will have another go in the morning.' More muffled murmuring and then Boland leaned in and said, 'We are going to Melbourne and will be back at dawn. Back in the van for you lot.'

We were locked in the back of the van again. Miss Gibbs asked them for some light as it was pitch black in the van. Eastwood opened the back door slightly and reached an arm in, where he struck a cigarette lighter. It gave us some faint light for a minute. He then threw a pillow and one blanket in. Miss Gibbs asked if we could keep the transistor, but Eastwood said, 'No. It is hot, and they will be able to trace us.' His parting words to us were, 'We will be back. Don't do anything stupid, like try and escape.' With his departure, the cigarette lighter also departed and we were left in pitch black darkness. They drove off, but a few minutes later they returned. Both men were walking around the van and there was banging and rustling. It sounded like they were securing something.

Miss Gibbs, probably speaking her thoughts out loud, said, 'Oh God, I hope they haven't planted a bomb!' It was the first time I had heard her voice break and quaver. I thought to myself, *I hope they haven't either*. We all curled up next to each other. We must have all dozed off, probably due to exhaustion and stress. It was cold, dark and very, very uncomfortable. Dawn broke and we were all tired, hungry, cold, and bursting to have a wee.

Search Headquarters – Faraday Primary School – 6.00 am

Dad was down at the school at the search headquarters, trying to help with the search. If he kept busy and kept moving, he didn't have to think and, being a Howarth, the fallback position was to show no emotion no matter what happened.

He overheard the searchers and police speaking in low voices, and a suggestion was made that when day breaks, they would need to start draining wells, dams and other water ways, looking for bodies. The group of men looked startled as they realised Dad was in earshot of the conversation but they thought he must not have heard them.

As he approached the group, he said, matter-of-factly, that he would be off home and if there was any news, he would be at the dairy farm, milking the cows. The search party breathed a sigh of relief and one of the men said, 'Glad the poor bugger didn't hear that we were planning on looking for his girls' bodies in the bloody dam.'

He did hear, and that morning he milked the cows with tears running down his face. Even his favourite cow, Bessie, gave him no comfort.

30

The escape

Miss Gibbs had barely slept at all that night in the cramped cold van. She must have looked around at her six charges and pondered. They had told her they would be back in the morning and to stay put. If they returned and found she had tried to escape, was she signing a death warrant for us all?

The alternative: what if they didn't come back? No water. No food. In the middle of dense bush, with no one knowing where we were. Locked in a van. If we were unable to get out, we would perish. She made her decision. Even though she was young, she was a woman made of stern stuff. And to do nothing was not an option. She took a long breath and put her plan into formation.

Miss Gibbs looked around and tested the panels, tapping on each one, at the side, on the floor of the van, on the back door panel. She kept going back to the back door panel and pulled at the chain adjacent to the back door. She asked for our help. Chris and I took turns in holding the chain, so she could lean on us for support. She started kicking at the backdoor panel. I felt bad as I didn't think I was much help; I couldn't maintain my position for very long for Miss Gibbs to lean on, but Chris was better and able to hold onto the chain for longer periods and give some support. Miss Gibbs, with her knee-high boots with good-sized heels that all our mothers secretly coveted, started kicking. She kicked and kicked and kicked. When she needed a break, we took turns to kick the panel, but really, we did not have the strength to make much difference.

We were all worried about what would happen if the men came back and saw what we were trying to do. Suddenly, one of the panels started to give way and Miss Gibbs redoubled her kicking efforts. It became more lose. We all stood and watched as a glimmer of fresh daylight came through the panel. It increasingly loosened and started to bend outwards. Suddenly, there was hope that we would escape our prison van. Miss Gibbs managed to kick it out. She was finally able to lean out and unlock the van door, and we all clambered out. We all quickly scampered to relieve ourselves behind various trees before coming together again. We were now really scared. What if the men came back? They would be so angry with us. We hadn't followed their rules and we had not stayed put. And being country kids, we always followed the rules.

Miss Gibbs drew us in close and let out a deep breath. She asked us to all keep together, to be very quiet and to follow her. We were going to try and find someone to help us. She appeared to be limping. All that kicking must have hurt her foot. If we heard a car, we were all to separate and run very quickly and hide in the bushes. She led the way down a track, getting further and further away from the van. We were all silent and trying really hard to make little or no noise with our feet as we picked our way through the dense scrub. We seemed to be deep in a forest surrounded by trees, dense bushes, fallen down logs, and rocks. Finally, we found a track.

The track was really hard to walk along, especially in summer sandals. I kept stumbling and getting small stones in my sandals and had to keep stopping to take my sandals off and remove the small stones. We followed along as best we could, walking as fast as we could from the van. Miss Gibbs would suddenly stop and raise her hand for us to stop. She would stand very still and listen. If she heard something, she would wordlessly gesture for us to separate and hide in the bushes. We would all run and scramble through the bushes, all trying to find a safe hidey hole, not all together, but not too far apart. My heart was beating so fast and so loud, I'm sure they would have heard my heartbeat. My hands were sweaty, and it made it hard to grab onto bushes to hide behind. With my eyes screwed up tightly, I kept praying to God, 'Please don't let them find us. Please don't let them find us.'

We were starting to get knocked about quite a lot. Our arms and legs were scratched with all the brambles and thorns we were running through. We were trying to find an easy track out, but we kept tripping over rocks and skinning our knees, too frightened to let out an 'Ouch.' We were getting further and further away from the van, but no closer to a town. Then the track started to widen and it became a little easier to walk. Our pace started to pick up.

All of a sudden, we heard gun shots. The sound of someone shooting. We all stood perfectly still, staring at Miss Gibbs. *Oh no!* I thought. *The kidnappers must have come back with their gun, and they are hunting us.'* Miss Gibbs frantically and silently beckoned for us to run and hide. We all separated and scampered to different hiding places in bushes and behind trees. I fell over and scraped my knee. It was bleeding, but I did not feel it in my hurry to hide. Miss Gibbs slowly emerged from her hiding spot and stood really still, head tilted, listening intently. More gun shots followed. We all cowered in fear, but she did not. She stood a little straighter, as though she had made a big decision.

We all heard voices laughing and talking. One was a lady's voice. Miss Gibbs beckoned for us to remain hidden, and slowly and cautiously she made her way towards the female's voice and disappeared from our view. In our hiding spots, we could hear the murmurings of a conversation Miss Gibbs seemed to be having with the lady, and then Miss Gibbs suddenly called out in a loud voice, 'It's okay. You can come out now.' I peered out from behind my tree and saw Miss Gibbs standing in a group with two men and two ladies, and she seemed to be explaining something to them. They looked very confused, and worryingly, the two men had guns.

All around me the bushes and trees started rustling. Chris stepped out from behind a neighbouring tree. Linda made her way out of thick bushes. Jill had found herself a really good hidey hole behind a large rock but she slowly emerged. Denise and Helen, being so tiny, were hiding near each other in the undergrowth. They stood up. I too, stepped away from my hiding place behind a tree. We all gathered in a group and came face to face with two men and two ladies, who just stood and stared at us with their mouths open. They seemed to be looking us up and down with a look of confusion and bewilderment on their faces.

I glanced down and for the first time I noticed that my hand and fingernails were filthy. My hair was tangled and felt really gritty. My knee was cut and bleeding. My legs were covered in dirt. There were twigs and grass on my cardigan. I looked over at Jill. Her face was covered with dirt. Her hands and fingernails were also filthy and there were prickles in her jumper. I then glanced at Denise, who looked really white faced and she was shivering. She had dirt all around her lips and her jumper and slacks were covered with grass stains. We looked really dirty and terrible. No wonder the other people could not believe that we just appeared out of nowhere in the bush.

The men with the guns quickly put them down and we soon realised, looking around and seeing lots of dead rabbits, that they were rabbit shooting. We were so happy that they did not want to shoot us. They were kind to us and kept asking if we were okay and what they could do to help. Miss Gibbs asked if they could take us to the nearest police station. A discussion ensued among the adults as to who should accompany us to the police station as no one seemed very keen to stay behind in case the kidnappers reappeared.

A decision was reached that we would all go together in one car, so we all piled into the sedan type car—five adults and six children. We climbed in the back seat. It was very squishy, and the adults asked us to sit on floors and knees and keep our heads down again in case the kidnappers reappeared. Even though it was very cramped and uncomfortable, for the first time in many hours we started to feel safe. We arrived at the township of Lancefield and pulled up outside the police station.

One of the men went into the police residence to tell them they had the kidnapped teacher and children in their car. I would later learn that the policeman in charge of this station, Senior Constable Anderson, was not at home, but his wife and son were. Mrs Anderson was a feisty small woman, who assumed that the rescuers were the kidnappers. She marched out to the car, peered in and saw us all squashed in the back of the car, some of us on the seats, some of us on the floor, white faced and filthy. She glared at our rescuers and started screaming, 'You should be ashamed of yourselves. What were you thinking? How could you do this to a young woman and six little girls?' The rescuers looked quite taken aback and one quietly said, 'Well, we thought we were being helpful.' This started Mrs Anderson off again. In a very high-pitched scream, she said, 'You call this helpful? Helpful? You wait until my husband gets home. He will arrest the lot of you.'

Meanwhile, before Mrs Anderson strode out to the car, she had organised with her son to load the shotgun and position himself at an open front window, with the gun trained on the car. Mrs Anderson had given him strict orders of, 'If they drive off, shoot the tyres out.'

Everyone started talking at once, and this time our mouths dropped open. Mrs Anderson was a fearsome sight. This very tiny lady, in the grips of absolute fury, directed at our rescuers. Finally, Miss Gibbs was able to explain that these were indeed the rescuers, and not the kidnappers.

Mrs Anderson calms down and apologises to the shooting party, who were Alan and Patricia Hayward, Ray

Butterworth and Anne Foster. Their weekend of rabbit shooting was dramatically interrupted. She then turned towards the police station and started waving her arms around. She called out, 'You can put the gun away now. You don't need to shoot the tyres out.'

We caught a glimpse of a young man (Mrs Anderson's son) at the front window with a gun aimed at the car.

31

Chaos and confusion

The Andersons contacted D24, telling them that we had been found. A brief respite. The house was warm. We were offered food and hot milos. As we all sat on the couch and sipped our milos, Mrs Anderson clucked over us and gently wiped our filthy faces with warm, wet face washers. Six exhausted, pale-faced little girls and a young, female teacher, remarkably still calm, although a little dishevelled.

The respite was very short lived. Mr Lindsay Thompson (who was both deputy premier and education minister) arrived with his entourage of senior police, and very soon more police kept arriving. I had never seen so many police—ever. Mr Thompson was concerned and very kind.

At the same time, the press descended and set up outside. There were people everywhere and for a time, it was bedlam. There was so much noise outside and voices calling out, 'Where are they? We need a photo! Can they be brought outside? We need to meet our deadlines. Are they hurt? Have they been attacked? Is an ambulance coming?' I was really puzzled. Were all these people talking about us? *Why do they want a photo of us? We are really dirty and haven't brushed our hair or cleaned our teeth. And our clothes are grubby.* I peeked out the front window and there were people everywhere, setting up large cameras and microphones. Mainly men. Surely not to see us?

I was taken away from my sisters to a quiet room and formally interviewed by Inspector Russell and Detective Senior Sergeant Coates. A statement was compiled at 10.50 am. I tried very hard to tell the policemen what had happened.

The voices from outside became louder and more insistent. 'When do we get to see them?' We were confronted by shouts of, 'We want a photo. We need a photo. The public want a photo.' So, a short time later, we were escorted outside with Miss Gibbs and Mr Thompson and photographed in a group. As we got outside in the bright sunshine, we were all quite shocked at the number of reporters and camera men all clicking away on their cameras. We stood there as a group, patiently having our photos taken. And then some of the reporters, who were all men, started calling out to us, 'Did they hurt you? What did they do to you? Have you got any injuries? Were they violent?' and, 'Do you miss your mum and dad? Did you think you would be killed?' I started to feel really scared again and when I looked around, everyone in our small group was looking worried and scared. It was a relief to go back into the police station where it was warm and safe.

A little while later, I went outside the police station to the back garden by myself to get some fresh air, but mainly to try and make sense of what was happening.

I was thinking how odd this all was and found solace looking at some flowers in the garden. I jumped back as a man approached me with a notebook and a strange look in his eyes. For a start, he was very friendly, but in a way that made me feel uncomfortable. He started asking my name and what grade I was in at school. Those butterflies in my tummy came back. Mum and Dad always told me not to talk to strangers, but he seemed to want to be my friend so I told him my name and what grade I was in and that my favourite football team was Richmond. He seemed really interested and started writing in his notepad. He was staring at me but not in a nice way. So, in a conversational tone, he said, 'Did the kidnappers hurt you?' I didn't know what to do or say to that question, so I looked down at the ground, hoping he would go away.

But he kept going. 'Come on, you can tell me. Did they hit you? Did they push you? Did they scare you?' I still didn't know how to answer, and I had no words to describe what had happened to us. He was scaring me with all these questions. Undeterred, he continued questioning me. 'Your knee is bleeding. They pushed you over, didn't they? Is that how you cut your knee?' He sounded really excited and happy about my bleeding knee. I finally looked up at him and in a quiet voice, I said, 'I fell over. I tripped on a stump in the bush and cut my knee.' He replied quickly, but his voice was filled with disappointment. 'Oh, is that all?' and he walked away. I stood there thinking for a few minutes and felt very sad as I then realised he wasn't my friend. That man wanted me to be hurt as it would have made a more exciting story for him and his newspaper.

We were separated from Miss Gibbs, who was taken away to give a detailed statement. She was still very composed, but pale. We were going home! We were split up into two groups and led to waiting police cars. In the first police car were me and my sisters, and in the second, Chris, Linda and Helen. We were on our way back to Castlemaine Police Station to be reunited with our families. A lot had happened since we set off for school the day before.

32

Reunited

It was pretty exciting to be driven back in a police car. The police were very kind to us and gave us ice cream, even though it was still morning and we never got to eat ice cream in the mornings. We arrived at Castlemaine Police Station and there were people everywhere. A large crowd had formed on the street in front of the station.

As the police car came to a stop, we opened the car doors to jump out, but the police beat us to it. They quickly surrounded us, screening us from the crowd, who seemed to want to reach out to embrace us, and quickly hurried us inside.

Again, there seemed to be lots of people inside the building—lots of police in uniform looking very stern and worried. I couldn't see Mum and Dad for a minute, but I knew they were there as one of the policemen had told me they were waiting inside for us. I suddenly saw them towards the back of the room. Dad, in particular, was acting very oddly. He looked worried, pacing up and down at the back of the police station He saw us and marched over to us like he was in the army. He shook each one of us by the hand, but his hands were shaking.

Then, all of a sudden, he stepped back and started to cry. He hugged us all to him really tightly as though he would never let us go.

It was then, seeing Dad break down crying in front of people, that I started to grasp the enormity of what was happening. Mum was very white faced, shaking and sobbing, and she kept hugging us. There was more sobbing, then she would hug us again and sob some more. By this time, we were starving and just wanted to go home. As we were leaving the police station, a photographer snapped a photo of Mum carrying Denise out, holding her very close with a look of such anguish and relief on her face that captured the moment perfectly. That particular photo was picked up by overseas newspapers, and that photo went around the world. We received lots of lovely letters from people in other countries. One very kind lady from America sent us six gold crosses, which were very special to us.

We all ventured out of the police station to go to our cars, and chaos reigned once again. I found myself surrounded by press with cameras and microphones. I was separated from my family, and all these men were calling out to me, all at the same time, calling me by name. 'Robyn. Over here. Robyn. Look this way. Did they hurt you? Were you scared? Did you cry? Did they hit you? Did they tie you up? Tell us more. Tell us more.' *This is odd, I wonder how they know my name*, I thought.

The second car pulled up with Chris, Linda and Helen alighting from the police car. All of a sudden, I was alone and they were surrounded by the same people that were so interested in me moments earlier. I tried to sneak through the throng to say hello and ask them how they enjoyed the ride in the police car. I wanted to check if they got ice cream too, but I could not get through. One of the men pushed me aside in his eagerness to get closer to the other girls. One minute I was the centre of attention, the next, I was discarded.

33
The police investigation

Huge relief for the police. The hostages were free with no loss of life. But the public were horrified and outraged, and the police knew they had to catch the perpetrators quickly. Saturday was a sunny, warm day with thousands of people flocking to Melbourne to watch the VFL Grand Final between Carlton and Richmond at the MCG. For the police however, it would be a weekend of hard work and painstaking investigations.

Thanks to Mary Gibbs, they now had two vital clues. They had a detailed description of the two kidnappers, and they had the van with its registration number, HOC339, which Mary Gibbs took careful note of. A check with the motor registration branch showed that it belonged to Tip Top Bakeries of 170 Edward Street, East Brunswick. Melbourne based detectives had a lead they could follow up on and did so straight away.

The descriptions of the two kidnappers were sent to every police station in the state. Police were ordered to drop everything and check for possible sightings of the duo. At 2.00 pm, police at Kyneton decided to conduct a thorough search of the outlying Cobaw ranges. In charge of this team was Detective Inspector Keith Platfuss, a very experienced policeman, who had vast knowledge of hardened criminals. Platfuss was pretty sure one of the kidnappers was Pentridge escapee, John Eric Taylor, a man who had spent most of his life around Castlemaine and Bendigo. Platfuss radioed D24 and requested six carbines. He informed D24 that he had information that the offenders were in the Cobaw ranges. 'I am trying to get aircraft for search. Request carbines and ammunition.'

At 3.20 pm, a light plane carrying armed police took off. At the same time, police received a tip that the kidnappers were in a car going towards Horsham. They blocked all the roads within a fifty mile radius of Horsham.

In Melbourne, detectives raided houses in Elsternwick, Richmond, Ivanhoe, Coburg, Brunswick, and Noble Park, looking for Taylor. In the next ten hours, they would receive reports that Taylor was in Kilmore, Colac, Rochester, Boort, Birregurra, and Yarram. He was everywhere and yet nowhere.

But it was in Melbourne at 3.30 pm that the first real breakthrough occurred. It was to do with the red Tip Top van. Detectives had learned that the van did not belong to Tip Top. Instead, it had been sold to a used car dealer in Brunswick, who had sold it to a Mr Cobb only a week earlier. Police had the salesman looking through mug shots of known criminals at Russell Street. They were off to a good start.

Throughout the Saturday and Sunday morning, the entire Victorian police force worked together to try and bring about an early arrest. This included the CIB, uniform, communications, country, and metropolitan. It

THE POLICE INVESTIGATION

felt personal as the victims were indeed the community's victims and it was an attack on innocence and a way of life.

At 3.00 pm on Sunday afternoon, Assistant Commissioner Miller called a press conference and released an identikit drawing of the two kidnappers and the van that had been brought in Brunswick ten days earlier. There was still much angst and fear in the community, and Mr Miller was aware that he needed to be calm, succinct and measured in his press conference. While reassuring the public that all that could be done to catch the perpetrators was being done, in reality the only decent lead so far was the sale of the red van.

After the press conference, Mr Miller called a meeting with senior police and senior politicians to discuss a reward. They all agreed that it was imperative that the government should offer one. But how much? It was eventually decided that $50,000 would be offered. Mr Miller wanted to offer $100,000, a sign perhaps that he really didn't have much to go on. The meeting broke up and everyone decided to call it a day—except for Mr Miller. 'I'm going to D24. I've got a feeling I need to be contactable just in case.'

The unofficial grapevine within the criminal underworld had been working overtime and Mr Miller had been quietly reaching out to all his contacts to come forward with information.

A short while later, a call came through at D24. It was from a man claiming that he had been an accomplice to one of the kidnappers in a previous crime. He said he had valuable information, he wanted the reward, and he also wanted indemnity on some hold up he claimed he had pulled with another man, who he would name as the kidnapper. The hold ups were at some Melbourne bayside railway stations. Mr Miller believed him and arranged a private meeting.

No honour among thieves, but in another sense the whole community, including the underworld, were outraged about this crime against children and wanted them caught. So perhaps there was. That evening, Mr Miller met the informant alone and received the vital information that he needed. He was told the two men involved were Clyde Boland of Bendigo and Ted Eastwood of Edithvale. Mr Miller found him to be credible. Apparently, this man went by the name of Jim Fontaine, and he had been approached by both Eastwood and Boland to be a part of the kidnapping, which he declined.

The weekend after the kidnapping – safe at home!

It was a surreal weekend as we had a house full of visitors. Not as you might think, friends and relatives, but the press. And as we lived on the Calder Highway, we were easier to find than the other families. Most of the major papers were represented and as was the custom in the bush, if someone came to visit, you invited them in and offered them a cup of tea. So that is what Mum and Dad did, totally unprepared for the onslaught as they chatted to us all. They took photos, chatted some more, drank tea, took notes, and took more photos. I was getting tired of all these strange people (journalists), mainly men. I went up to our lounge room to read my Enid Blyton book and curl up in the comfy lounge chair, and some of the men followed me and started picking up the family photos on the mantelpiece, taking notes while talking to

THE POLICE INVESTIGATION

each other. Then they would wander back to the kitchen and come back again with another cup of tea and a piece of cake (that Mum had baked for *us*). They would then start going through all the photos again. I didn't like them touching our photos.

It was most odd, and I found I couldn't concentrate on my book. And I was getting cross. Our heads were spinning, and Richmond had lost the VFL final—to make matters even worse. We had never had so many visitors in our lives! Grandpa and Grandma McInnes drove down from Bendigo, looking very worried, and didn't eat any of Mum's cake, which she kept offering. They seemed very keen for us all to go outside to play. I was very keen to hover around the door and eavesdrop, which I did.

Grandma McInnes kept asking Mum if we had seen a doctor and if not, Mum really needed to make appointments. Mum kept saying to her Mum that there was no need as we had come back unharmed. Grandma McInnes was very keen for us all to go to the doctor—especially me—and be thoroughly checked out all over. She kept mentioning it over and over. 'Iris, they need to see a doctor and have a full physical assessment, just to make sure.' Mum kept asking, 'Make sure of what, Mum? They have not been harmed.' I peeked through the door and Grandma looked like she wanted to cry. Mum looked puzzled. Grandma then started behaving very strangely, gesturing towards the door and making funny hand signals, trying to alert Mum that I was listening. I would later learn that Grandma McInnes was very worried that we had been sexually assaulted, and that me being tall for my age at ten, I would have been at particular risk.

34

Catch those madmen

'They must be caught' was the mantra that weekend. Every news bulletin was running the same story—two mad men on the loose must be brought to justice.

One of the lead detectives on the case was Reginald Baker. At that time, he was Detective Sergeant Reginald George Baker, who would eventually climb to the rank of assistant commissioner. He was a kind and caring man, with a calming manner. A slightly built man with glasses, he ensued a studious air. Dad, when first meeting Reg, would ruefully lament to Mum and us kids, 'Well, he's a pretty skinny sort of a fellow. Not much brawn about him. Seems too polite for a copper. I suppose he knows what's he's doing, but I don't know how he would drag the crims to the ground!' But that would become a familiar refrain in the years to follow Detective Sergeant Reginald George Baker. Dad, whenever he would find a mention of him, on whatever case he was involved in, in the newspapers, would always give him his full title as he would regale us with a snippet of Reg's amazing detective ability.

I had the pleasure of meeting Reg and his lovely wife, Jessie, a few years ago to speak to him about the Faraday

Kidnapping and he was still kind and very generous with his time. Reg told me that as a young sergeant he was quite nervous about being assigned to the task forces to apprehend the kidnappers. He was told it was going to be a very dangerous assignment. Reg had three young children of similar ages to myself and my sisters, so I have always thought the case for Reg became very personal.

Two task forces had been established—one to be deployed to Edithvale, Melbourne, and the other to Bendigo. Reg was assigned to the Edithvale task force, where he was told that Eastwood, a karate expert, would be armed with a gun under his pillow and the arrest would be fraught, dangerous and probably violent. They made their preparations fully armed at 4.00 am. They stormed into Eastwood's flat in Edithvale and grabbed Edwin John Eastwood. At the same time, the other task force stormed into a house on Queen Street, Bendigo and grabbed Robert Clyde Boland. By 4.30 am Monday morning, they had them both.

Reg and the team found Eastwood at 4.10 on Monday morning, asleep in bed with his girlfriend, Rita Healey. He was arrested quickly and did not offer any resistance. He said, 'I've been expecting you. I know what this is about.' The police task force was relieved as they had expected this to be a difficult arrest. A thorough search was done of the bedroom while Eastwood and Ms Healey got dressed, and various items were taken as exhibits.

Eastwood accompanied the police outside the house, where a Holden sedan (HEM110) was parked. Eastwood, when asked, confirmed that it was his car. A search was made of the car and various objects were discovered, which included a transistor radio and a silver watch. Eastwood was then quizzed about these items and said they were identical to items that had been described by Miss Gibbs as belonging to the kidnappers. They also told him that he met the physical description of the kidnapper, who was armed with a sawn-off rifle.

In conversation, Detective Sergeant Reginald Baker casually asked him what he had done with the gun. He said, 'It's in a creek somewhere near Heathcote.' Reg was dumbfounded. He then went on in a puzzled, non-threatening tone, 'So, you admit that you were one of the two men who kidnapped a teacher and six students last Friday from Faraday State School. Is that correct?' Eastwood replied, 'Yep.' Eastwood was then taken to the homicide squad offices and placed in an interview room. It was 5.15 am. Eastwood then piped up and asked, 'What's this about the Woodend caper? Did they really take the money up there?' The policeman guarding him replied, 'Well, you should know. You made the phone calls.' Eastwood replied in an aggrieved manner, 'No. That was some other criminal bastard trying to get in on the caper. You can't trust anyone these days.'

Monday 9 October 1972
Monday evening. We were all crowded around the telly, listening to the nightly news bulletin as we were made aware that there had been an arrest. Brian Naylor, the newsreader on *Channel Seven* announced in a grim voice that police had arrested two men in relation to the Faraday Kidnapping. Edwin John Eastwood, twenty-one years old from Edithvale; and Robert Clyde Boland, thirty-two years old from Bendigo. Mum went very white and spoke in a strangled voice, 'Oh my god, that's my cousin's son. Robert Clyde Boland is a relative.' The room went really quiet, and Dad said, 'What a bastard!'

35
You can choose your friends, but not your relatives!

To explain further, my grandfather, William McInnes, was the second youngest of eight children raised in Redesdale Victoria. There was quite a big age difference between the youngest and oldest siblings. Christina, my great-grandmother, had been widowed at a young age and life was difficult on the farm at Redesdale. Grandpa used to go out and shoot rabbits for their food, and also to sell to supplement their meagre income.

One of Grandpa's older sisters was Maud, who had married into the Boland family of Bendigo. She and her husband had three sons, one of whom was Rueben Boland, the father of Robert Clyde Boland. Mum had never met Rueben or his family as the two branches of the family had drifted apart, as often happens with large families. However, this dubious family connection did cause a lot of consternation in my mother's family, especially for my maternal grandparents. Grandma and Grandpa McInnes were gentle people, who were very well respected in Big Hill. Happy to potter in their garden,

Grandma would play the organ at the local church, with Grandpa taking a keen interest in the VFL. They enjoyed family time spent time with their daughters and their families and there was never any conflict—well, only that once over politics.

They then found themselves in a position of distress, upset that their granddaughters had been kidnapped, upset that the perpetrator was a relative, and upset that they lived in the same area as the Boland family. Bendigo became too small for them all for a number of years. They were taken aback by the conduct of Rueben Boland and his supporters, who were shouting from the roof tops that his son was innocent. It was a witch hunt and whatever the cost, he would get him off. They were frightened for themselves and us.

The Boland family were a well-known Bendigo family and up to this time, quite well respected. They ran very successful plastering businesses. This changed after 6 October 1972, and feelings ran high against the name Boland for many years. I discovered later that the Boland plastering businesses lost customers as people refused to deal with them. Socially, many of them were ostracised, even those who were very distantly related to Rueben and his son but shared the name Boland.

It has always been somewhat disconcerting that the kidnapper and I shared the same great-grandparents. A very odd twist of fate. But neither Rueben Boland or Robert Clyde Boland showed us any compassion or concern and ensured the trauma kept being repeated over and over with numerous criminal trials.

The long road to justice
Sunday 8 October

City Watch House: Robert Clyde Boland was unshaven and barefooted when he was brought into a makeshift court at the City Watch House in the late afternoon. The 'court room' was the police canteen, and the presiding Justice of the Peace, Mr M E Costello, sat at the kitchen table between a refrigerator, a stove and a water urn.

Boland had been interviewed at length but had refused to answer any questions. It took six minutes to remand him to stand trial on seven charges of having taken away the teacher and the girls with intent to gain advantage for himself or other persons.

Later that evening, it was Eastwood's turn. This time it took two minutes to remand him on the same charges. Eastwood however, had given a full and frank admission to the police.

I never quite understood why he was so open. Part of me likes to think it was a guilty conscience and he wanted to do the right thing; the other part thinks, *Nah, personality disorder with the need to brag.* At that time in his life, he was only twenty-one. I don't think he was truly bad yet. Mad maybe. But the badness would manifest later with more crimes, including another horrific crime against children.

Tuesday 10 October

The public got their first look at the two accused at the Melbourne Magistrate's Court bail hearing, which was packed with the press and interested bystanders. The hearing was heard before Chief Stipendiary Magistrate, Mr W J Cuthill, with Mr Frank Galbally appearing on behalf of Robert Clyde Boland, and Barrister Mr Brendan Murphy, appearing on behalf of Edwin John Eastwood. Both men had obtained the best defence lawyers at that time, and the police were aware that they needed to be very clever about how they would proceed with the bail hearing. I can only surmise that both the men's families (probably parents), definitely in Boland's case, were funding their defence.

The usual procedure in serious crimes is for the application for bail to be heard in chambers, closed to the general public and press. The police, however, were very confident with their case and had decided not to argue too strongly for a closed hearing. They were aware that if it was heard in open court, the press could report on the case. In a plea for bail, Mr Galbally claimed that his client was innocent, that he was a respectable married man, and lived in Bendigo with his wife and four children.

Mr Murphy, when seeking bail, said, 'There is no evidence of Eastwood being convicted of violence in the past and without bail, he would have difficulty preparing a defence.' After the charges were read out, Mr Murphy told the magistrate, 'There is considerable amount of public hysteria about matters on which the accused is charged. The evidence today should be heard in public for the benefit of the accused. There is a sinister connotation attached to chamber hearings.'

Inspector Griffith, who was the police prosecutor, said, 'We are asking for bail to be refused, having regard to the serious nature of these crimes. I have evidence ready. It can now be heard in chambers.' Mr Galbally said, 'I am not concerned in the slightest with the nature of evidence. Boland proposes to plead not guilty, and the onus is on the police to produce good reasons why bail should be refused.' Mr Cuthill, SM, said, 'Bail applications in serious matters before the Supreme Court are not heard in open court.' Inspector Griffith remained silent.

Mr Galbally said, 'That is news to me. I have always disputed that with you. Accounts on bail are reported in law reports and newspapers. I want my client dealt with calmly in an orderly way. Boland's bail hearing should be heard in open court.' Mr Cuthill looked towards Inspector Griffith, who continued to remain silent. Mr Cuthill said, 'Alright, we will hear the evidence now in open court.' The police were very happy with this ruling as the press would have full access to the arguments.

Detective Sergeant Reginald Baker took the stand, was sworn in and said, 'It is alleged Eastwood is a married man with a child, living apart from his wife and child. He is living at his parents' home. It is alleged he has made full admissions and signed a record of interview in which he said ….' Mr Galbally said, 'I object. He is going to say something somebody else has said. This would not be evidence against my client. He was going to say Eastwood has said something about my client.' Detective Sergeant Baker replied, 'Yes.' Mr Galbally said, 'I object because it is not evidence to my client.' Mr Cuthill said, 'What Detective Sergeant Baker was about to say is now to be left out.' The sergeant went on, 'It is alleged both men talked over a plan about six to seven months ago to kidnap a teacher at a country school and the children in the school, then take them to bushland near Lancefield. It is alleged the teacher and the children were to be placed in a trench to be dug in the ground and covered by galvanized iron with dirt placed on top. They were to be chained up and padlocked with plaster over their mouths.'

There was a gasp of horror from the gallery and momentary silence as people digested the enormity of this horrific plan. The press couldn't write fast enough in their notebooks, and there were horrified looks all throughout the packed court room.

Mr Murphy said, 'Is this evidence against my client?' Detective Sergeant Baker said, 'This is evidence of the plans.' Mr Murphy said, 'It should be limited to what happened. Matters raised in relation to the case are able to be published.' Mr Cuthill said, in an exasperated voice, 'This is the very reason I wanted the hearing in chambers. You don't know what you are going to get in evidence being given.'

Detective Sergeant Baker had a quiet moment of satisfaction when he looked over to the faces of the defence counsel. Mr Murphy and Mr Galbally then realised it was a big mistake demanding that the evidence be heard in open court, as it was both damming and truly horrific. And the press was going to have a field day. Mr Murphy said, 'Have you heard the name Jim Fontaine referred to in this case?' Sergeant Baker said, 'Yes.' Mr Murphy said, 'I put to you that you have received information from a person who, it would appear, had an intimate knowledge of the details of this operation. That information was given to you on the condition that this person did not appear in this case, and you paid him $3,000.'

Inspector Griffith interjected and claimed this suggestion was not relevant to the case. The magistrate agreed and ruled that this line of questioning was not relevant to the case. After a forty-five-minute hearing, bail was denied.

36

The line-up

Robyn - October 1972

My police statement reads:

On Tuesday the 10th October, 1972 I went to Russell Street police headquarters on the seventh floor. I there saw a line of men standing against the walls. At 11.41 am I identified a man in this line of men. The man I picked was one of the men that came to our school, on Friday 6th October 1972, and took us away in a red van. I was unable to identify the other man. Such a simple statement that does not give a hint of what was a truly traumatic experience.

My reality as a ten year old:

I felt sick. Butterflies in my tummy. *What if I get it wrong? What if I can't pick them out? Does that mean these bad men will go free?* All these thoughts and fears running through my head, in a jumbled mesh of confusion.

I was led into a room by three policemen. It felt so big, and it was empty except for the men. At the back wall, it was filled with men standing with their backs against the wall. They were so tall and big. They were all staring down at me, unsmiling, with grim expressions on their faces.

To the right, another wall. More men. Again, their backs to the wall, all staring at me. All waiting. To the wall on the left, there was one man leaning against the wall. He was not standing like the other men. He was different. He was a long way from the rest of them. *Is he even part of the line up?* He was slouching and half turned away and looking down at the ground.

He looked familiar, but the hair was wrong! *Don't make a mistake, don't get it wrong. Oh no! I think it could be him, but is he even part of this line up thing?* I wasn't sure. *Don't make a mistake!* My thoughts were getting very muddled and there was no one I could ask. I thought he was one of the kidnappers, but something about the hair colour was not quite right. I didn't want to make a mistake, and I was too scared to ask if he was actually part of the line-up. I wasn't sure what I was to do, but one of the policemen asked me to walk closer to the men and see if I could recognise anyone. I didn't want to. This was so horrible. All these men.

I walked slowly up to the back wall. I was so close, and all these men were staring straight ahead. There he was. He was in the middle, and he had a strange grin on his face. He pointed to himself and mouthed, 'Pick me.' My finger was trembling, but I raised it up and pointed at him. He was so close. It was Edwin John Eastwood.

I kept glancing over to the man on his own. This time he had his arms crossed, leaning against the wall, turning away from me, looking very relaxed. I turned back to all the other men who were standing up straight and tall and staring ahead. What to do? What to do? If I picked him and he was not part of the line-up. Maybe he was a policeman, although he needed to stand up straighter if he was a policeman. Would I get into trouble? He looked like the kidnapper, but the hair was not quite right.

At ten years of age, I had no experience of wigs, hair dye or police line-ups. I walked out of the room feeling worried that I had only pointed out one kidnapper.

The man trying to pretend that he was not actually part of the line-up was Robert Clyde Boland. I have never understood why he was allowed to stand so far away from the other men, in a slouched position—a much different posture from the other man. To this day, I still kick myself for not picking him out. I would later learn that Miss Gibbs had picked both men out.

37

One week after the kidnapping

October 1972

The week after the kidnapping there was a meeting of all the families and the education department called to discuss the future of Faraday State School. It was held at our home, and the press were there, still drinking cups of teas, still eating our cakes, still taking notes, and still taking photos. They had almost become part of the furniture as there was still huge interest in this case. The parents, with the recommendation from the education department, decided to close the school.

Dad was still keen that the school should stay open and continue but he was in the minority. The school would close, and we would all be sent to Harcourt State School. Faraday State School 797 was no more, and I would not realise it then, but it was also the end of the Faraday community as we knew it.

The school acted as the gathering place for the community, a place where families and neighbours would gather for the annual school Christmas tree concert, where dads would meet at the school for regular working bees, and the mums would see each other daily and chat at the school gate.

Those days were now over and the school would invoke a feeling of dread, sadness and fear that for me would take years to fade, and for Mum it never did. That simple act where three young mothers gathered at the school gate to collect their children one spring October day to be confronted by the unimaginable.

No more would children run out to meet their mums at the school gate, and no more children's laughter in the school grounds with games of chasey and hopscotch.

Just a single blue stone building, a beautifully built building, a solitary presence, with no more children to educate, whose purpose and reason for being was taken in a most cruel manner.

The whole school … well, all ten of us … were transferred to Harcourt Primary School approximately three miles towards Bendigo. It was a much bigger school than Faraday and for a short time we were a bit of a novelty and the Harcourt kids seemed to really want to be our friends.

38

Two weeks after the kidnapping

Annual school sports - Faraday Primary School 797
Late October 1972

It would be the last time we would come together as a school and march proudly under the Faraday school banner. We were all so excited to see each other again.

We were all in our lemon and white sports uniforms and came equal fourth with Strathlea, which was a very good effort considering our sports training had been interrupted.

We had a most successful day out, and our names were even in the Castlemaine Mail, which was thrilling for us.

First place U/11 80 metres - Robyn

First place U/11 hurdles – Lee. She was so excited as she had been practising really hard.

First place U/8 - hurdles - Jill

First place U/7 - 40 metres - Richard

We were so busy congratulating each other and jumping up and down that in all our excitement we didn't notice the police presence positioned just behind the Faraday Primary School 797 banner. How sad that there needed to be a police presence, in rural Victoria in 1972, at the school sports, with eyes trained and alert for any hint of danger to the students of Faraday 797 and their pretty, dark-haired teacher.

39
Oh no, not Melbourne!

We had been advised that committal proceedings were commencing at Melbourne's City Court on Wednesday 22 November 1972. Mr Howse was the crown prosecutor, Mr Brendan Murphy would be representing Eastwood, and Mr Frank Galbally would be representing Boland. Hearing the case was Mr JL McArdle (S.M.). I had been officially called to be a witness in the upcoming court proceedings as had Miss Gibbs and Christine Ellery.

Oh no, not Melbourne. Such a long way away and how were we ever going to get there? Dad started losing his mind about having to drive to Melbourne.

Leading up to this day, there was a lot of conversation around the kitchen table about the impending trial. It was a very big deal going to Melbourne—quite torturous, in fact. We would always be asking, by the time we got to Elphinstone, 'Are we there yet?' 'How much further?' Elphinstone was approximately four miles away from our home. It seemed such a long way. No air conditioning, no freeway, a slow car, and a cranky, nervous Dad driving.

Then there was the worry of where we had to go, if we would be able to find City Court, where we would park, how we would get there. Dad studied the Melway Maps for days on end and decided to park at The Royal Children's Hospital Melbourne and catch a tram in. In true Australian male fashion, he would always be really stressed about which tram to catch but would never ask for directions or help.

There had been a lot of talk and extensive press coverage about the case and the fact that Mr Galbally was representing Boland. He was, at the time, one of the leading criminal barristers. Dad was worried, so I was as well. Dad would often remark in a gloomy voice, 'That Galbally. He is always getting those bloody crims off.' I was really nervous about this Mr Galbally. Would that mean the kidnappers would be let go and try again to kidnap us? That would be so awful and wrong.

That particular trip was uneventful. Dad took me down and we parked, as planned, at The Royal Children's Hospital Melbourne. So far so good. Somehow we managed to get on the right tram, and we found our way into Russell Street. The problems started when Dad was getting off the tram. Dressed in his Sunday best suit, with his favourite Sid James type hat on, his hat blew off his head and blew down Russell Street. That particular day, Russell Street was congested with cars and trams. Dad took off and proceeded to run very fast down Russell Street. He was dodging trams, cars were tooting at him, and he was weaving in and out of the traffic, until he caught up with his hat which, at this stage, was in the middle of the road. He proudly returned, hat in hand, oblivious to all the curious stares he was attracting. I thought to myself, *I don't think people in Melbourne chase their hats.*

I was still really nervous and scared of Mr Galbally as Dad had told me he would try and trip me up over my evidence. But he didn't. He was actually pretty nice. But it was very daunting being confronted with barristers, solicitors, court staff, judge, police, and a packed courtroom. They all looked very serious. I had never seen so many people in one room.

I did my best to speak clearly and loudly so they would all hear me. But my voice sounded wobbly. And I was distracted by the sight of the two kidnappers. I kept staring at the two accused men. They were both in the dock, in suits, with their hair neatly done and their faces freshly shaved, looking like normal men. Looking around them confidently, they smiled at their families and supporters. *This is all wrong*, I thought to myself. *Why are they not dressed in the same clothes they were in when they took us, then everyone would see how scary they actually are?* They were pretending, hiding their true selves behind new clothes, shiny shoes and new haircuts. In that courtroom, there was nowhere for me to hide. I was still prey.

40
Detective Sergeant Reginald (Reg) Baker's story

Reg, in 1972, was at the beginning of his career. But even then he had something special. He would rise through the police ranks and eventually become an assistant commissioner of the Victorian Police force. Reg had an inquisitive mind—a mind that could absorb and remember detail. And he had a calm, gentle manner, which made people, even hardened criminals, want to confide in him. He was the perfect detective to arrest and interview Edwin John Eastwood.

I felt privileged when Reg graciously shared his memoirs that he had written in recent years. He highlighted important cases he had worked on, of which the Faraday Kidnapping was one—and a case he always remembered.

Reg had often attached correspondence he had received while investigating certain cases. Included in his memoirs were often thank you cards. What struck me though was that they were often from people he had investigated and charged with crimes. They would thank him for his decency and compassion towards them.

Of course, there was also many from victims/survivors of crime, all so grateful for his kindness and compassion, and for going that extra mile to ensure a conviction. As I mentioned earlier, Reg had been very apprehensive about being assigned to the task force to apprehend Eastwood, and he was surprised and relieved at how easy it had been.

During the interview, Eastwood made a full admission. He named Boland as the other perpetrator and signed a record of interview. Reg was quite surprised at how forthcoming Eastwood had been. Eastwood also made admissions regarding his involvement in an armed hold up at Cheltenham East Post Office about two to three weeks earlier, where he used the same sawn-off rifle that he used in the kidnapping. Eastwood was quite chatty and appeared very keen to tell the story. Reg, being a thoughtful and methodical interviewer, was able to elicit a lot of information and commented at one stage to Eastwood, 'This crime will be known as the crime of the century', which encouraged Eastwood to elaborate even more.

Reg realised that the more he stroked this young man's very distorted ego, the more information he was getting. He made sure to let him know that he would be well known in the course of history. Sadly, he was right.

As one of the lead detectives on the case, Reg shared his interview notes and evidence he complied. I have added some thoughts and insights that I learned as part of being an unwilling participant in the whole sorry saga.

Edwin John Eastwood met Robert Clyde Boland on 29 May 1972. They met at a five-day training course at the Gyprock Plaster Training Centre, Abbotsford.

DETECTIVE SERGEANT REGINALD (REG) BAKER'S STORY

Eastwood had learned karate and had stickers on his car advertising that fact. He was keen to make a lot of money and the post office robberies he had been indulging in were not going to finance the lifestyle he dreamed of. Reg formed the view that here was a young man, twenty-one years of age, filled with bravado, easily influenced, and already drifting into a life of crime—which he was bragging about. Boland approached him while they were attending the plastering school, complimented him on his karate skills and suggested that he was a man who could handle himself. They started cultivating a friendship and Boland asked him if he would be interested in joining forces in an illegal enterprise that would net them a lot of money—a million dollars. The enterprise would nett Eastwood half a million dollars. He was hooked, and the thought of all this money overcame any pin pricks of conscience that may have occurred.

Robert Clyde Boland from Bendigo had been planning this type of crime for some time but had just not found the right accomplice … yet!

Eastwood then became a frequent visitor to Bendigo to see his new business partner and discuss their new venture. It was Boland who came up with the idea that they would kidnap a teacher and pupils from a small country school and demand a million-dollar ransom, which they would split half each. Boland suggested that Eastwood, now an avid devotee, go and watch the *Dirty Harry* movie by Clint Eastwood, to get ideas so they could fine tune their plan. He did this and became very enthused. The *Dirty Harry* movie included a sequence where Harry had to go to several telephone boxes to deliver ransom money, making it impossible to follow him with back up.

Eastwood, on his many trips, had already found a school that he thought would work well for them. It was secluded and set off from the Calder Highway. Both men agreed that this school had potential and was their best find so far, so they decided to undertake surveillance of the school.

Of these many meetings, one was held in Melbourne, where Boland stayed with Eastwood at the Mentone Hotel in September 1972. Eastwood then drove Boland back to Bendigo. On this trip, his girlfriend, Rita Healey, was in the car as was another man—probably Jim Fontaine. The three men were openly talking about the planned kidnapping. Boland asked Eastwood how much she knew—meaning Miss Healey. Eastwood replied, 'Nothing.' Boland then turned to the woman and snarled, 'For your own health, the less you know the better.' After this meeting, they decided they needed a van to convey hostages to a secluded location in bushland near Lancefield, where they had chosen to hide the victims. Boland would organise the van. He made inquiries with Phillip Kaufman of Bob Jane's car yard in Richmond, and Stewart Innes Motors of Bendigo regarding the purchase of a Kombi van or similar vehicle.

He then obtained a loan of $400 from Carway Finance Company in Bendigo on 23 September 1972 and used the money to buy a red Thames van (registration number HCC339) from Ronald Vincent at Brunswick on 3 September 1972. Boland gave the name of Brian Cobb and signed the receipt, B. Cobb. He then drove the van to Bendigo and parked it in the streets around Bendigo. It was seen on Edward Street, Bendigo by Mr Harold Mullen and Reverend Tudball-Smith between 1 and 4 October 1972.

On 6 October 1972, Eastwood drove to Bendigo in his Holden sedan, arriving at 7.30 am. Boland then joined him and they drove to bushland off Feeneys Lane, Lancefield, where they left Eastwood's car. Boland then drove Eastwood, in the red van, towards Faraday and at about 10.30 am they were hailed by Lynton Ferris on Lancefield Road near the Calder Highway, to assist him with a bogged vehicle. They were unable to drive Mr Ferris' vehicle out of the bog, but they did drive him to a nearby farmhouse to obtain assistance. This is important as Mr Ferris would become a witness for the prosecution.

They arrived at Faraday Primary School at 1.35 pm and kidnapped a young female teacher and six female pupils, leaving the ransom note in a desk. Once they reached Lancefield, Eastwood drove to Melbourne, leaving Boland to guard the seven hostages. At 4.40 pm, Eastwood made a phone call from a public telephone box to Wayne Grant of the *Herald Sun* newspaper, informing him of the kidnapping.

Eastwood organised notes to be pinned under shelves in various phone booths around Melbourne with directions using a Morgan Street directory. He had left the street directory at the tally-ho boy's home in Burwood, near the front gate, with the intention that Reverend Father Oakley would collect the ransom money and take it from one telephone box to the next. Eastwood would covertly observe Father Oakley and collect the money when it was safe to do so, just like in the *Dirty Harry* movie.

At 7.25 pm, he placed the phone call to Lindsay Thompson, but panicked when he was not put through straight away. He then called Father Oakley, who was unavailable. He was fearful that a trap had been set, so he collected and retrieved the street directory and returned to Lancefield with some potato chips to eat.

At 2.00 am on Saturday morning, the two kidnappers decided to abandon the hostages and leave them locked in the van. The two men told the hostages they would return in the morning at dawn. Eastwood drove Boland to Bendigo and on the way, disposed of the sawn-off rifle over the McIvor Creek, south of Heathcote, as well as a bag containing padlocks, chains and other articles used during the kidnapping, at a bridge over the Campaspe River at Axedale. At Bendigo, Boland gave Eastwood a bedspread and left him to sleep in his car at the rear of 165 Queen Street, Bendigo (Boland's home address).

After the confession was received, Eastwood accompanied Reg and other detectives as well as the police photographer and the police forensic scientist, to back track along his movements. Reg then took Eastwood through his statement as they stopped at the various points. 'Would you show us where you disposed of the sawn-off rifle and the bag containing the chains and other property?' Eastwood took them to the bridge over the Campaspe River at Axedale and said, 'I'm sure this is where I threw the bag away. We must have gone past where the gun is.'

Eastwood then directed the police crew to the left side of the bridge facing Bendigo and indicated a bag on the edge of an island in the middle of the river. He said, 'Oh, there it is. No wonder I didn't hear any splash.' The bag was recovered and the contents included a chain, padlocks, keys, some sticking plaster, gloves, a hat, a knife, and a couple of pieces of black cloth. It was quite an ominous find. The police photographer got to work carefully photographing the site, bag and all the items found.

Eastwood then directed the police back through Heathcote to a bridge over the McIvor River. He pointed out the location of a sawn-off .22 calibre rifle in among some reeds on the right-hand side of the road, again facing towards Bendigo. Detective Sergeant Baker then asked the question, 'Is that the sawn-off rifle you used in the kidnapping of the teacher and children at Faraday?' Eastwood agreed that it was.

Detective Sergeant Baker removed the magazine from the rifle and found that it contained five live rounds of bullets. The police then drove Eastwood to Faraday Primary School, where he took part in a movie film re-enactment, showing how he and Boland had kidnapped the teacher and the children. This re-enactment was also fully photographed.

The car was then directed to a track off Feeneys Lane, Lancefield, where Eastwood indicated a trench about 150 yards to the left of the track in bush country. The trench was about fourteen feet in length, about four feet wide, and about three feet, six inches deep. It appeared to be freshly dug. The trench was covered with galvanized iron lying on top of saplings, acting as supports. The iron was covered with soil and it had logs and branches on top. There was only a small opening on the track side of the trench, with a shovel left there.

Eastwood went on proudly to explain, 'That's the hole we were going to keep them in, but you can see up the other end it is starting to cave in, so we decided it wasn't safe. We were going to cover this end up with the sheet of iron over there, and nobody would know they were here.' He was immune to the looks of horror on the policemen and photographer's face.

Eastwood then directed the group back along the track about one hundred yards, near the base of a tree on the same side of the track that the trench was on. He pointed to a piece of soft earth and said, 'You'll find the wood from the gun about six inches down there.'

He helped the police to dig down below the surface of the earth with sticks, and the wooden stock and strap was recovered and carefully photographed. Eastwood then directed the police to a water hole in a paddock on the opposite of the track. As they walked to the water hole, he pointed towards a galvanized iron shed across the other side of the paddock. 'That's where I got the iron for the hole I dug,' he helpfully volunteered. He then went on to pinpoint the spot where he threw the rifle barrel into the water. It didn't take police long to locate the barrel with the aid of the shovel taken from the trench site.

The group returned to the homicide squad office and Eastwood was taken to his home at Edithvale, where more items of property, connected to the kidnapping, were taken into possession. Eastwood was then charged at the City Watch House with seven counts of kidnapping.

Detective Sergeant Reg Baker had just worked thirty-five and a half hours straight. He slept well that night, satisfied of a job well done.

It was such a matter of fact telling of a tale borne from greed and evil. Could they have really gone through with this vile plan?

I have always liked to think that they could not and they had a skerrick of decency left. They were both fathers themselves, with young children, but I think deep down in their planning and scheming the end result was to leave no living survivors. And that was certainly the view of the judge at the end of the trials.

After the kidnapping, some months later, Dad and Senior Constable Anderson of Lancefield had formed a friendship. We had been invited to visit Senior Constable Anderson in Lancefield, and Dad was very keen to go. Mum was less so and she declined the visit. I was very keen to go as well, probably due to the fact that we didn't really go many places and to be invited to visit a policeman was very exciting. After a lot of nagging, Dad finally agreed that I could tag along and then after more nagging from Jill, she was allowed to come along as well.

The visit started off very well. We met him at Lancefield Police Station with Senior Constable Anderson genuinely pleased to see us. He seemed very happy that we appeared to have no ill effects from the kidnapping. The two men were having a great chat about the kidnapping, subsequent arrests and police investigations. Senior Constable Anderson then asked if we would like to visit the crime scene. Dad was very keen so, of course, we were as well.

What an adventure! Dad was very careful to keep up in our car as we followed Senior Constable Anderson in the police car. We drove out of Lancefield for a few miles and headed deep into a forest, following a windy, bumpy track with the trees and scrubs becoming denser and denser. We came to the gate, where many months before we were captive in a back of a van and ordered to face the other way as our captors drove us through. We came to the clearing, our clearing, where we were forced to play a treasure hunt—the most miserable treasure hunt of my life. It felt sad. This place seemed alien and the echo of fear still resonated.

This adventure started to not be fun at all and I could not understand why my tummy felt like it had dropped to my boots. I started to feel sick. Senior Constable Anderson looked like he was really enjoying showing Dad around, explaining lots of details to him with lots of nodding and gesturing. They then veered away from the clearing and left the track, heading off into the bush. Dad called out to stay put, but I did not want to stay behind with Jill so I slowly followed them. I was puzzled to see them both leaning over something. It looked like an old, rusty piece of iron and there were some logs lying on top. As I got closer, I saw it was a long, dug-out trench with an opening at only one end. The two men seemed very interested in this trench. Their faces were grim and they were talking softly to each other and shaking their heads. I just stood and stared. That was where the kidnappers were going to put us—in a cold, dark, muddy trench. That image of the trench would continue to haunt me for many decades to come.

There would be times in the future when I would be battling mental health issues brought about by undiagnosed PTSD. I was angry at both those men, especially Dad, for taking me there that day. But as the years have passed and wisdom is gained, I realise neither those two men, especially Dad, were acting with malice. It was more a misguided enthusiasm for a crime and event that had such a huge impact on all of our lives. Back then, so very little was known about childhood trauma and its effects.

As a maternal and child health nurse, I was fortunate to be employed by Macedon Ranges Shire Council in 2018 and work with a fantastic team of nurses in the most beautiful part of Victoria, where Lancefield is located.

Lancefield today is a vibrant, picturesque town, with wide streets reminiscent of times gone by, a bakery to die for, wonderful dress shops, and a bookstore with a very eclectic range of books that encourages one to spend a very long time browsing, and maybe even buying, more books. It is a place I would love to spend more time in.

Families with young children are moving to this area due to its proximity to Melbourne, but also the opportunity it provides to raise their children in a rural environment.

As part of my role as a maternal and child health nurse, we visit families at home after their baby is born. Whenever I was booked to visit a family with their new baby at their home, my heart always sank when I saw the address was Lancefield. It is such a pretty town, with lovely families looking after their babies beautifully. The home visits were always a delight. Why then was I so anxious to venture into Lancefield? It is only now that I have realised I will forever associate Lancefield as the place where I first saw my grave as an eleven year old.

41

Trial no. 1 - a blunt trauma

Tuesday 6 March 1973

The trial begins for the two accused men, Edwin John Eastwood and Robert Clyde Boland, at the Melbourne Supreme Court. The trial was being heard before Mr Justice Gowans. The crown prosecutor, Mr Howse, appeared for the crown. Mr Austin Asche QC, with Mr Brendan Murphy, appeared for Eastwood; and Mr Charles Francis QC, with Mr John Dee, appeared for Boland. Both men pleaded 'not guilty' to all charges.

I was relieved as Mr Galbally was no longer representing Boland. Dad said that was very good for our side. I was also very puzzled as Eastwood had originally confessed to the crime and in the line-up he said, 'Pick me, pick me!' and now he was saying he was not guilty. This court business was a very strange business, and one I didn't understand.

The crown had a very strong case and the trial attracted huge interest, with packed galleries filled with the general public and press. The key witness would be Mary Gibbs, and Detective Sergeant Reginald (Reg) Baker would organise the witnesses and also be called to give evidence himself, due to his arrest of Eastwood. They also had fingerprint evidence and a signed confession from Eastwood.

Miss Gibbs was always called before us and the press would make a lot of fuss about what she was wearing each day she attended court to testify. There was always photos of her in all of the major papers with a running commentary of her outfit, colour, cut skirt length, what shoes she wore, and the handbag she was carrying as she entered and exited the court building. She was usually on the stand for at least two to three days. We never heard her evidence. We were all on tenterhooks waiting for the call to come though that we must attend the Supreme Court in Melbourne so I could testify. The call came though, and Dad lost his mind about the drive to Melbourne. He started pouring over maps and Melways, trying to work out the best route, where to park and what time to leave.

Mum was preparing his best Sunday suit (his only suit) and his Sid James type hat (his favourite hat), and after many hours fretting, the day before the big drive to Melbourne, he would decide (as usual) that we would drive and park at The Royal Children's Hospital Melbourne and catch the tram into the Supreme Court.

As usual, he would not ask for directions from anyone. It was always a very stressful time standing at the tram stop with Dad muttering and swearing under his breath, trying to read the tram timetable and trying to work out which tram to catch. We usually managed to get the right tram, more by good luck than any skill on our part.

We made it on time, and the courts were packed. There were people everywhere—well-dressed men and women, and the press and the judiciary, in their attire of gowns and wigs, with an air of learned superiority. Dad and I were two country bumpkins, out of our depth on every level. The police were very kind and courteous, and Detective Sergeant Reg Baker would always come and say hello and check in on us. Dad would then tell me again that he still didn't think he had the physique to tackle the crims to the ground, but he seemed a pretty clever fellow all the same.

Miss Gibbs would already be in court giving evidence. We would not be allowed inside, so would be waiting outside. The hours would drag and the butterflies in my tummy would get worse. Christine, my friend, would be there as well, with her parents. We would all sit together, waiting and waiting in a small room on the side of the main chamber, to be called in. I was gobsmacked the next day to see the newspaper coverage, where there would be a picture of both Christine and I with a detailed description of what we were wearing as we were entering and exiting the court building. In my case, it would be my Sunday best—a very inexpensive outfit bought in Castlemaine, or a dress made by Grandma.

Christine had been called into the courtroom to give evidence, and I knew I would be next. All of a sudden, I started squirming in my seat, busting to have a wee. I whispered to Dad, 'Dad, I have to go to the toilet.' At this stage, we were in a foyer area with lots of people milling around. Dad gets in a flap as he cannot spot a policewoman to take me to the toilets, and he did not want to let me go in by myself. 'Dad,' I said, 'I am busting, I have really got to go.' At this point, I noticed a blonde-haired, well-groomed lady watching us, who had clearly overheard my plea. She came over and said to Dad, 'I will take her if you like.' *Phew!* I thought. *That's good.* Dad looked at this woman in horror and said in a loud voice, 'You bloody well will not!' *Oh no!* I slink down in my chair. *Oh no, Dad. People are staring at you again. They will be thinking you are a rude, grumpy Dad.* The blonde lady walks off, and Dad spies a policewoman. He organised with her to take me to the toilet. When I returned and sat back down, Dad said to me, 'Do you know who that blonde lady was?'

'Nup,' I reply, 'But she was trying to help me,' I said in what I thought was a helpful tone. 'Help you? Help you?' splutters Dad. 'It was that bloody kidnapper's wife. Boland's wife.'

Dad was still muttering to himself. 'Bloody nerve. Bloody cheek. Mmm.' She smelled of cigarette smoke and I am now glad Dad did not let her take me to the toilet. But she looked sad, as if she could shatter into a million pieces. She wore lots of makeup and she had teased blonde hair and a fixed smile on her face, like she was holding everything in place.

42

Reliving the crime over and over

My name is called and it is my turn to give evidence. I was really scared and nervous. I didn't want to mess up my evidence. My footsteps echoed on the wooden floor of the courtroom, and it seemed to take an age before I reached the witness box, where I had to climb up steps. I could smell lemon scented furnish polish, used on the mahogany wood. I looked up and they were staring straight at me—the two accused men. I felt sick. I was not sure where to look—at the judge, looking extremely grand with his wig and gown, who is high above me on my right, or the jury to my left, a mixture of men and women. No one was smiling.

I looked straight ahead and there, sitting before me, were tables of men in wigs and gowns. There were so many of them, and they seemed so serious and stern. They were the prosecution team and two teams of defenders for the two accused. I took my oath on the Bible and swore to tell the truth. I looked up at the galleries and they were filled with the press and members of the general public. They were all staring at me, all waiting for me to speak—the young, country bumpkin in another frightening and alien environment, giving evidence at the Victorian Supreme Court in Melbourne.

Mr Howse, the prosecuting counsel, takes me through my evidence. He was kind, and I relaxed a little. The opposition counsel stood up to question me. They were kind also. I was wary as I didn't want to make a mistake. During this exchange, they asked me about the identification parade and said I had only identified one man. I pipe up that I thought that there was another man who looked like the older kidnapper there, but he was standing apart from the rest of the men and I didn't think he was part of the line-up. They were not interested in this, and simply pressed on with the fact that I had only identified one man. Mr Howse stands again and asks me to go through my impressions of the line-up. He asked me why I didn't identify the second man. I was pleased to be able to tell him as I had always kicked myself for not pointing him out. It was over and I was so relieved and tired. I stepped down from the witness box and looked to find Dad. I took my seat next to him.

Suddenly, there was a huge development in the case. Edwin John Eastwood had changed his plea to guilty! He had stood up and declared to the packed gallery that the trial was a farce and he was being used as a patsy and wanted to change his plea to guilty. The judge urged him to speak to his legal counsel and ordered a short adjournment. After the adjournment, a guilty plea was entered. The case against Robert Clyde Boland would continue as he continued with his not guilty plea.

43

Do not vomit

We decided to wait around after I had finished testifying as Eastwood had been called by the prosecution as a witness and we wanted to hear his testimony. Dad and I thought this would be the last time we would have to come back to the Supreme Court.

We were both really relieved; Dad because he did not have to drive to Melbourne again, and me that I did not have to testify again in such a grand, unfamiliar environment with all these serious, learned people looking at me. I thought to myself, *Eastwood will take the stand, tell the truth and it will be all over. They will go to jail and we can go home.*

It was very crowded in the gallery, and Dad and I somehow managed to get a seat upstairs in the front row. We didn't have to wait long. As Edwin John Eastwood was called, he strode in very confidently. He was wearing a suit and his black hair was all slicked back. He refused to swear an oath on the Bible. *That's odd*, I thought to myself. There was complete silence in the gallery as everyone was waiting to hear what he would say. The prosecution asked him to name the other man involved in the kidnapping and he refused. He was asked again and he refused. Eventually, he was ordered to name his accomplice, and was asked if he was in the room. He hesitated and slowly reached into his pocket and pulled out his glasses, which he put on. Slowly looking around the room, he studied all the faces for a few minutes and then slowly, in a clear voice, he said, 'No, your Honour. He is not here.'

As he started to speak, my brain felt like it was going to explode, and I wanted to stand up and shout, 'No. No. No. Why are you lying?' *This is so wrong*, I thought. *You shouldn't tell lies.* I could feel the bile coming up my throat. It started to feel swollen and I started gulping and swallowing. I was going to be sick. *Don't throw up. Don't throw up*, I kept saying to myself. I had to place a hand over my mouth as I had visions of vomit dripping over the balustrade and landing on the floor of the court chamber.

Eastwood then proceeded to give evidence in a very theatrical manner, where he claimed that he had been forced to sign the confession by corrupt cops, who had threatened his girlfriend. He claimed that his accomplice was not Robert Clyde Boland. When asked who his accomplice was, Eastwood dramatically paused, screwed his face up as if in deep thought, shook his head, rubbed his eyes, and slowly announced to a hushed courtroom that it would be Meggise. 'Ginger Megs,' he announced proudly. 'That's what I call him because of his red hair.' The prosecution barrister then asked in a very grumpy exasperated tone, 'Does Ginger Megs have a name?' Eastwood sighed and didn't talk for some minutes. He then said, 'David O' Ryan.'

Eastwood testified that they had asked Clyde Boland if they could use his garage to park the van for a few days before the kidnapping, but he had refused. It was put to Eastwood by the prosecution that his story was a complete fantasy as it had been made very clear what would happen to him in Pentridge for dobbing in Boland. Needless to say, Eastwood would never be called again as a prosecution witness. But it was far from over for us all.

On Friday 16 March 1973, Eastwood appeared in court to be sentenced. His defence counsel asked Detective Sergeant Baker if Eastwood had made any statement of penance regarding the crime. The detective relayed to the court a conversation that he previously had with the defendant. Eastwood said, 'You know, we could never get away with this.' Detective Sergeant Baker said, 'Why?' Eastwood said, 'Everyone must have been praying for those little kids.' Detective Sergeant Baker said, 'Why do you say that?' and Eastwood replied, 'Well, everything just seemed to go wrong. I'm sorry, and I'm glad nothing happened to them.'

Edwin John Eastwood, aged twenty-two years old, was sentenced to fifteen years hard labour and it was directed that he served ten years before parole. Justice Gowans said he had not considered ordering a whipping because the victims had not been ill-treated, but he went on to say that this kidnapping, directed at children, was at the lowest level on which kidnapping could be carried out.

44

A good copper

Detective Sergeant Reg Baker had to endure a robust cross examination when he was giving his evidence regarding the arrest and subsequent confession of Eastwood. He explained, calmly and matter-of-factly, the details of the arrest and the ease with which the confession was obtained. He denied that he coerced or threated the convicted man.

He was then able to produce to the court a tape of the confession he typed, word for word, over five hours. Everything Eastwood had said, he then asked the accused to read it back to him, to make sure he had got it right. Eastwood was happy to oblige and, unbeknown to him, he was recorded reading back the statement.

Mr Francis, the defence barrister, attempted to ridicule this account, insinuating that no one could type for five hours and have one hundred per cent accuracy in transposing another person's account. Reg agreed that Mr Francis was correct, as he was sure that in the five hours he did miss one word, but only one word. Dad, when reading this exchange in the paper the next day, roared with laughter. 'Well, he may be a skinny fellow with no brawn, but by gee he is a clever bugger.'

Miss Gibbs's testimony
I never heard Miss Mary Gibbs give evidence, but my understanding was that she was calm, measured and rock solid in her evidence. She had identified both men and would spend hours and days in the witness stand, giving evidence and being subject to lengthy cross examinations.

At one stage, she was continually asked by the defence counsel how she could be sure she had identified the right man in Boland. She replied, 'At one stage, he took off his glasses.' She was standing quite close to him and had studied his profile carefully, already planning in her mind that if we survived the ordeal, she would need to give a good description of the two men. The defence counsel then instructed Boland to don the hat and glasses that had been seized and alleged that this was the disguise used. Upon seeing Boland in the disguise, Miss Gibbs leaned back in the witness chair, gasped in fear and covered her eyes. 'It is definitely him,' she told the hushed court.

The trial commenced on Tuesday 13 March and would end on Saturday 7 April. The Crown had prepared carefully and were confident that they had an airtight case. But they would come up against a formidable foe in Robert Clyde Boland's father Rueben, who would never concede that his son was guilty and was prepared to make sure he had the best defence possible.

The investigation had been thorough, and an array of witnesses were called to testify to Robert Clyde Boland's guilt. Some workmates, ex-plasterers, would be called to testify that Clyde, as he was known, in the months leading up to the kidnapping, would often speak about kidnapping someone famous and ask for a ransom of $1 million. At the time, his workmates did not take him seriously, but after the events of 6 October 1972, they came forward and gave testimony.

Rita Healey, Eastwood's girlfriend, who referred to Eastwood as Ted, would testify that the two men were meeting regularly, and that one time they were talking in riddles in a car driving to Bendigo, where Boland asked Ted what she knew. 'Nothing,' the younger man replied. Clyde turned to her and said, 'The less you know, the better for your health.' She would recount in court that he was talking like a gangster—Al Capone style. The defence counsel suggested that the only reason Ms Healey was testifying was that she had been granted immunity from the theft charges she was currently on, and that her testimony was not credible.

Mr Ronald Vincent identified Boland as the person that had purchased the van, and Mr Ferris identified Boland as the driver of the red van, who assisted him with his vehicle that was bogged near Lancefield the morning of the kidnapping. Also, a fingerprint had been located on the driver's side door of the van that was a match for Boland. Boland's defence was that he was working for his parents on the day he was supposedly purchasing the van, and they provided an alibi for him that day.

Of the day of the kidnapping, he was supposedly in Melbourne, parked in a car with a woman he was allegedly having an affair with. The woman could not be found to verify this account. Regarding the fingerprint on the van, he claimed he must have leaned against the van when Eastwood and Fontaine paid him a visit, asking him to store the van in his shed on Sunday 1 October. The crown was very strong in countering these claims. They stated that the woman he was having an affair with was a fictional character as she would have appeared by now, and the appropriate time to name her as an alibi witness would have been on the day of arrest, not months later.

The crown provided expert evidence that any fingerprint placed on the van at the time alleged by the accused could not, having regard to the weather prevailing between 1 and 6 October, have been as clear as the print discovered on the van on the morning of 7 October. The Crown was confident they had refuted all the claims made by the defence counsel.

The jury retired to consider its verdict on Friday 6 April, but after nineteen hours and forty-four minutes, they could not reach a verdict. At this time, this was the longest jury retirement in an Australian criminal case, that involved one accused. We were all devastated. My family, Miss Gibbs, the police, we were at a loss as to how this outcome came about. It was rumoured that there had been jury tampering and Robert Clyde Boland was released on bail. There would be another trial. It was not over. *It's not over. I have to go back to court*, I thought to myself. And worst of all, he was out on bail. What if he came back and tried again? He knew I had testified against him. He would be angry. What if he came back and killed us all? He knew where we lived. My thoughts were all in a muddle. We knew he was guilty.

In those next few months, I started to feel really funny—and scared. Nowhere felt safe. Not home, not at my new school, and especially not when we were out shopping in Castlemaine. We knew Boland had returned to Bendigo. I had butterflies in my tummy all the time, and I kept seeing guns and knives popping up in my mind.

Everywhere I went, I kept seeing men with red hair, or men wearing sunglasses and/or a hat, which set my heart pounding, my palms sweating and a feeling of dread would descend. I was on edge all the time, continually looking around, expecting to be stabbed or shot. One day, Mum took me shopping in Bendigo. A special treat. I had really been looking forward to this as I was getting a new dress. We were walking along Pall Mall when I saw him. He was wearing the same sunglasses, a hat, and he had red hair. He was staring at me and crossed the road. He started walking closely behind me.

The feeling of dread built up and I thought I was going to be sick. I stopped suddenly and stood still. I closed my eyes and hoped it wouldn't hurt too much. I waited for him to stab me in the back with the knife. The man frowned at me as he side stepped and kept walking. It was not the kidnapper. He did not have a knife. I was losing my mind. I was not sleeping very well, because I knew he was out there and we were not safe.

45
Trial no. 2 - repeat blunt trauma

June 1973
The second trial commenced and tensions in our little home rose once again. Dad lost his mind again about driving to Melbourne and poured over the Melways for days prior. He was stressing about the drive to Melbourne and where to park. There was a lot of conversation around the kitchen table about the best way to go, what time to leave and how long it would take so, as usual, we drove to The Royal Children's Hospital Melbourne. We parked in the car park and caught the tram in and by some miracle, we caught the correct tram. This time Mum came along as well and Dad was much calmer at the tram stop.

We spent a lot of time waiting outside the court in the foyer area. Reg came along to say hello. He had been promoted to senior sergeant. Dad was quite chuffed about this and put it all down to the work he has done on the kidnapping. I was called to give evidence, and it was a pretty poor effort on my account. I simply wanted to forget about it and had trouble remembering. Dad told me after I had finished that I had stuffed it up.

TRIAL NO. 2 - REPEAT BLUNT TRAUMA

Rueben Boland was there. A fierce looking, red-haired man, father of the kidnapper, and cousin to Mum. I caught him staring at Mum, and then he walked over to the defence team. They conferred quietly and kept glancing over to us. The defence notified the judge and the prosecution that they had a new witness they wished to call. Her name was Iris Howarth. My mother was being called to testify for the defence. Mum was mortified and horrified.

She was called and swore her oath on the Bible, looking uncomfortable and anxious. The defence started questioning her about her relationship with the accused and the Boland family, and pointed out that she was closely related and indeed the accused was her second cousin. Mum pointed out, in a quiet, hesitant voice, that this was so, but she had never met him or any member of his family.

The defence counsel was quite sceptical of this and called for the accused's father to be brought in so that Mum could identify him. Mum did this and the defence pounced on it. 'So, how do you know who he is then if you have never met him?' Mum replied that he was pointed out to her in the foyer of the courthouse earlier in the day. And I thought to myself, *He stood there, staring at her for ages as well.* The defence was a bit deflated over this but undeterred, they carried on. 'So, Mrs Howarth, you grew up in the Bendigo region and are roughly the same age as the accused. So, it would not be unreasonable to assume that you attended the same secondary college as the accused, therefore you would have known him.'

Mum replied, 'No, I did not. I attended the Bendigo Ladies Secretarial College.' The defence soon realised that there was really nowhere to go with this line of questioning and they released Mum from the dock. Mum was very white faced and her hands would not stop shaking. Dad was really chuffed and regaled the story over and over for weeks to come. 'Ooohh, Iris. You got them a beauty. Those bloody upstarts. Trying to make out you went to the same local school as that bastard, Boland. No, not you. You went to a bloody private ladies' college. That fixed them right up. Those toffee-nosed bastards.' Mum was never called again to give evidence. Dad was always very disappointed that he was not called to give evidence but in hindsight, it was best he didn't.

This time the jury did not deliberate for as long, but again failed to reach a verdict. Again, it was rumoured that the jury had been tampered with, but the police did not have enough evidence to prove this. We were so disheartened and again could not understand that a verdict could not be reached. I heard Mum crying in the bedroom that night.

The kidnapping and subsequent trials were starting to take their toll on all of us. The trials kept making us relive the event over and over. We could not move on, and there was a real fear that Robert Clyde Boland would walk free. The press was ever present reporting the trials, with page-to-page coverage in all the major newspapers.

On a positive note, we had all settled into school at Harcourt Primary School. I started playing netball with the Harcourt Blue Wrens, and our social circle and sporting opportunities had widened.

46

The wife

October 1973

In 1973, an amendment to the Crimes Act had been brought in. It meant that the wife of a man charged with kidnapping could become compellable by the prosecution to give evidence in certain circumstances. This was a very important change to the law and would have ramifications for the case.

The prosecutor planned to call Clyde Boland's wife to testify for the prosecution, and she would be compelled to do so. Prior to this, she had refused to testify, claiming spousal privilege. So, for this next trial, Lois Boland, wife of Clyde Boland, would be called and had to give testimony on what she knew. She could not claim spousal privilege. Also, the police had become quite disheartened and dismayed at the outcome of the last two trials and retraced their steps and re-interviewed all of Clyde Boland's known associates.

They discovered a new witness—Frank O'Halloran from Bendigo. For reasons of his own, he had not come forward earlier. He had known Clyde Boland for approximately fifteen to twenty years, and their paths had crossed frequently when both were working as sales representatives for different companies in Bendigo. Mr O'Halloran would go on to testify in the third trial, that after Easter 1972 he was working at a local car yard when he was chatting to Clyde Boland. It became apparent to both of them that they were earning a lot less money than in their previous careers as sales reps.

The conversation then took on a more sinister tone, with Clyde Boland asking, 'Would you like to earn more money?' O'Halloran replied, 'Yes. For sure. What have you got in mind?' Boland said, 'It involves a large amount of money. More than you would ever get in a normal working life. It involves a million dollars.' O'Halloran looked surprised and said, 'What is it, Clyde?' Boland said, 'Kidnapping.' O'Halloran replied, 'Oh yeah. Pull the other leg, Clyde.' Boland retorted, 'No. I am serious.' O'Halloran said, 'You can count me out. I'm not interested.' Boland said, 'You have not been used to a lot of money. With a million dollars, you could live a good life. Get out of the country and start a new life.' O'Halloran said, 'Not interested. I am not that sort of fellow.' Boland would not give up. 'No, think about it. It's a good plan. It will involve the government, a number of people, a ransom, which we split 50/50, and you just have to live on your nerves for a couple of days. If we are caught, we would be granted a government pardon.' O'Halloran, in an exasperated manner, said, 'Why pick on me, Clyde?' Boland replied, 'I've known you throughout the rep days. You're a good type of fellow. Would be calm in a crisis. The right man for the job.' O'Halloran said, 'Not interested, Clyde.' Boland, still undeterred, said, 'Well, think it over and I will check with you in a few days.'

About two or three days later, Frank O'Halloran was approached again by Boland and asked if he had changed his mind. O'Halloran replied, 'I told you the first time, I am not interested.' Boland said, 'Okay then. I will see a couple of fellows in Melbourne.' Boland then followed up with a phone call to Mr O'Halloran at home later in that week, which he refused to take. He then confided in his wife about the strange conversations that had been occurring with Clyde Boland.

On the Monday after the news had broken about the Faraday Kidnapping, Mr O'Halloran confided in a friend, stating that he knew who had committed the crime. He detailed the conversations he had had previously with Clyde Boland. A week after the arrest, he also went and consulted with a Bendigo solicitor, requesting advice on what he should do. He was advised that it was his decision and one he had to make alone. Frank O'Halloran's wife, his friend and his solicitor all gave evidence at the third trial, verifying these conversations.

When asked, under quite stringent cross examination, why he had not come forward earlier, and had indeed only come forward when the police had visited him at home a few days prior to the commencement of the third trial, the reasons he gave included him not wanting to be involved, he had a sick young child requiring cardiac surgery, he had recently opened a business with another couple and did not want it to be known that he knew Clyde Boland, and that he thought there was enough evidence to have convicted him without his testimony. Another reason perhaps, was fear. Dad always described Rueben Boland as a hot-headed standover man in Bendigo, who people were frightened of. Or could it be that the Boland family were respectable businesspeople running successful businesses in Bendigo and that a fellow small business owner would not want to upset them?

It would appear that there were quite a few people in Bendigo who held information and knowledge that may have secured an earlier conviction. How does that make me feel? A little sad that they were happy to throw a young teacher and young girls into a continued media frenzy, reliving over and over the trauma by repeat testimonies at repeat trials. But in the end, they did all speak up and tell them what they knew, so mixed in with my sadness is gratitude.

At that time also, feelings were running very high, and the name Boland was synonymous with the Faraday Kidnapping. People were very angry and fearful that this crime had been committed against children. It appeared that any businesses in Bendigo run by various members of the Boland family suffered quite a downturn following the events of October 1972. Clyde Boland's defence had always consisted of alibis—on the day of the van purchase, his parents would vouch that he was with them in Bendigo.

On Friday 6 October, Boland himself would give salacious evidence that he was having an affair with a woman named Susan Buchanan as the sex life he had with his wife was poor. On the day of the kidnapping, he had gone to Melbourne to meet Susan and had parked at a beach, where they were having sex in the front seat of the car. This testimony was very titillating and provoked widespread press coverage and gossip, as was intended. Susan Buchanan never appeared in person at any of the trials and was never able to be found. The prosecution was scathing of this alibi and were convinced that this woman did not exist.

This time however, the jewel in the crown case would be the evidence of Lois Boland who, by this stage, had had enough. Hounded out of Bendigo, her four young children were traumatised, ostracized and living in poverty in a caravan in Geelong. She eventually needed to seek police protection. It was time for her to tell what she knew. The defence tried to make her out as a woman scorned, bent on revenge against her philandering husband. The truth, however, was much sadder and frightening, and it would highlight that there were many more victims than six little girls and their young teacher.

47
Lois' story

Lois had been a teenage mother. She was pregnant at sixteen. She would marry the father of her baby, Robert Clyde Boland, in 1959. They would go on to have four children together. The two youngest children were the same age as me and Jill at the time of the kidnapping. Money was tight, and Clyde struggled to hold onto a job. The Faraday Kidnapping thrust Lois Boland and her children into the full glare of the media and the condemnation of the Bendigo community, which would eventually force her and her children to leave the area.

It would appear that Lois was a victim of domestic violence, and at first she stood by her husband, not bringing herself to believe he was guilty. Also, Rueben, her father-in-law, could not accept any other idea than that his son was innocent and was going to beat all the charges. He was spending a great deal of money on a very skilful and effective defence team. Lois would attend each of the trials nicely dressed, hair dyed blonde and neatly set, and she appeared to be a dutiful, loyal wife. When she was called to testify in the first two trials, her evidence had been vague and she kept repeating that she would like to help, but did not know anything, Also, at that time, the prosecution could not compel her to give evidence against her husband as kidnapping was not a class of crime where the evidence could be compelled to be given so that conversations taking place between a husband and wife could remain private.

I don't really know, but I like to think that Lois was struggling with her conscience and the police paid her a visit to inform her that the Crimes Act had been changed, so she would now be compelled to tell the jury what she knew and was obliged to recount private marital conversations that she had with her husband. Clyde was running the defence that he was in Melbourne on the day of the kidnapping, conducting an affair—one of many he would claim he had been having as he was unhappy in his marriage. By the third trial, Lois and her children were living in a caravan at her sister's place in Geelong. The children were not coping. Life was tough and they were very poor. She had also been receiving threats and was trying to provide for her four children as a single mother, with limited job prospects. Whatever the reason, Lois Boland presented at the third trial and spoke her truth.

She took the stand as a witness for the prosecution. Lois Boland testified that during the course of the committal hearing in December 1972, she asked her husband if he had done it. He hissed at her, 'Of course, I did it. But I now know where I went wrong.' About his co-accused, Edwin John Eastwood, Lois would testify that her husband told her, 'Ted will be lucky to make it to trial for dobbing me in.'

On his whereabouts on 30 September, the day the van was purchased, Lois confirmed that her husband had travelled to Melbourne that day, and he was not in fact working at his parent's property, as stated by him. This was very damaging to the defence's case and they then went to work to destroy her credibility.

She would be subjected to a lengthy cross examination, where she was accused of being a jealous, vengeful woman, who had changed her evidence in a fit of pique as her husband was having an affair. In one disturbing incident, when being asked about the colour of her husband's eyebrows, she was asked to look directly at him from the dock, where he grimaced at her. The defence counsel, not content with this, decided it would be better if she examined the eyebrows in close range, and they received permission for the defendant to leave the dock and walk down to the front of the witness box. Husband and wife stared at each other for several minutes, until Lois then completely broke down and nearly collapsed in the witness box. The judge, witnessing the interaction between husband and wife, was so concerned with what he saw, he revoked Clyde Boland's bail.

In her own words:

Counsel said, 'What is the reason for your change in evidence?' Lois said:

> *During the last trial, I was extremely upset. Very, very upset. I didn't want to come to court. I didn't want to give evidence. I was heavily sedated. I wanted to get out and get home as quickly as possible. I had the children very upset. Just the whole thing was*

very unnerving. The children themselves have been persecuted. The children are being victimised. We are living in a caravan at my sister's. There were three adults and seven children, and it was extremely difficult during the hearing.

I was also working at the time, which made it even more difficult. During the first trial, I didn't pay much attention to what was going on. It was like it was happening to someone else. Then, after my husband told me about Ted, and then I heard them both give their evidence, and realised what they were saying was lies. I realised then it was all true what he was being accused of. I didn't want him near the children. I didn't want him near me. I signed the affidavit to protect my children. In my opinion.

I was scared silly, they sent me to a minister's residence when my husband was out on bail, as there was fear for my safety. Then when we came back, we had to have a policewoman staying in the house with us. The children were extremely bad. Then I received a book from my husband called, "Live while you are alive". I received a card calling me Judas, and then I was subpoenaed to give evidence and I am really scared. I am scared of him, and the only reason now I have got is, that by giving evidence he will get me anyway. So, I might as well go for …

She never got to finish her sentence as she was interrupted by the defence trying to close down these disclosures.

The defence was seriously concerned as Lois' testimony was very damaging, and they had not been able to paint her as the vengeful wife from hell. Instead, it was evident to everyone in the court that she was terrified of her husband. The defence counsel moved quickly to dismiss Lois from the dock but were thwarted by the jury foreman, who asked the judge if he could ask Mrs Boland two questions. The judge agreed to this request.

The jury foreman stood up and asked if she perceived the book, *Live while you are alive* a threat. She replied that she did. He then asked if, throughout the course of their marriage, her husband was a violent man. Lois replied, 'He was. I have seen him violent many times.'

Two questions the defence really did not want asked.

48
Trial no. 3 – repeated blunt trauma

October 1973

Here we go again! At least I get some days off school. The call had come through that I was needed to testify. And this time they asked for my younger sister, Jill, as well. As usual, there was a lot of consternation in our household about how to get to Melbourne. Dad lost his mind again about the drive. Melway Maps were brought out. Dad poured over them for days, with lots of conversations around the kitchen table about where we would park and, as usual, he decided to drive to Melbourne along the Calder Highway and park in the car park of The Royal Children's Hospital Melbourne. We would then catch the tram to the Supreme Court in William Street, Melbourne.

My sister, Jill, was only nine years of age. Far too young to be asked to testify, in my opinion. I remember seeing her white faced and very small in the witness box, recounting what she could of the events of 6 October. After her ordeal was over, the stress was too much, and my parents had to rush outside with her to get some fresh air, where she started to vomit in the gutter. This time I was better prepared with my evidence as Dad had got me to write down everything I could remember. But I was so very tired of it all.

It was all starting to get to us all. We were caught up in limbo, it always hanging over our heads. We were unable to move forward until there was a conviction. There was deep resentment in my family towards Rueben Boland and his son, for the continuation of the sad, sorry tale and their refusal to concede. We had to retell out story over and over to a courthouse that was foreign and scary to us. We feared he would be set free, and we feared there would be reprisals against us as we were thrust into this legal realm that we were all so ill-equipped to deal with.

The prosecution was very confident. The trial was going very well, and it was hard to see that this time the jury would not reach a guilty verdict. Each trial they had prepared extensively and had brought to the court compelling evidence for a guilty verdict. This time the evidence of Lois Boland and Frank O'Halloran had dealt the defence a crippling blow.

Also, several prisoners who had been in remand with Clyde Boland came forward with information that he had approached them seeking advice as to how to beat the charges and expressed his concern that the teacher could ID him. They had offered to testify for the prosecution.

On 19 November, eight weeks into the trial, a female juror reported to the court that she had received, at her home, a phone call from a man claiming to be speaking on behalf of the police. He told her she must find the defendant 'guilty' and that if she did so, she would receive $5,000.

Defence counsel immediately called for the jury to be discharged, stating that the jury might believe that the defendant was in some way responsible for this call and it might improperly affect the jury's verdict. The judge made the decision to continue, warning the jury that he was confident that the call to the juror had not come from the police, or the defendant and his associates. He suggested that there were 'cranks in the community who might have been behind the call.'

It was a clever ruling by the judge, and one that stood up at the later appeal. It was always rumoured that the call had originated from the Boland camp in the hope of having the jury dismissed. And we have always believed there was jury tampering in the first two trials. In my mind, it was the only thing that made sense when the evidence was always strong.

49

Is it the end?

Rueben Boland, successful businessmen in Bendigo, was married to Ivy, and he was the father of three sons. One of his sons was a serving policeman, and another was killed in a car accident at a young age. Rueben refused to ever accept that his son was guilty, and he spent a lot of time and money in trying to prove this. He was detested by my family and never showed any of us any indication that he had some type of understanding of the ordeal that had been inflicted upon us. He came across as a hard man, who was unyielding in his quest to see his son free. And that was his only focus, no matter the cost. There appeared to be very little or no support offered to his daughter-in-law and grandchildren, who had been forced to flee Bendigo and live in poverty in a caravan in Geelong.

As a son, Clyde really didn't measure up in his father's eyes. He was a teenage father, who had dropped out of school early. He was unable to hold a job for any length of time and he had four young children to support. He had, at times, worked for his father's plaster works, but Rueben was known to be very exasperated and was quoted as saying that his son was useless and he could never get a full day's work out of him. However, in the courtroom, evidence was given that he was grooming Clyde to take over the family business, which was ridiculed by the prosecution as a fantasy.

On 18 December 1973, the jury came back in with the verdict. They had deliberated for two hours and fifteen minutes, and in that time had taken a one-and-a-half-hour lunch break. 'Guilty.' Mr Justice Norris sentenced Robert Clyde Boland to sixteen years in jail, with a minimum of twelve years. In his summation, he said that he was convinced that Boland was the mastermind of the crime and had been properly convicted.

He also went on to add that he was convinced that he was prepared to murder his victims to escape prosecution. The crime was vicious, callous and bold, and all so that the defendant could have an easy life. The defendant showed little compassion to Miss Gibbs and the children, leaving them locked in a van on a cold night with no food and water, in a lonely spot in the bush, with only a bedspread for warmth. There had been no remorse shown, and if Miss Gibbs had not been the magnificent type of young women she was, who managed to keep calm and escape, one does not know what would have happened.

Was it over, or was it just the beginning?

50
Treading water

Teenage years—and what a bloody awful time that was. I am very glad to see the back of those years. The feelings of low self-esteem, desperately trying to fit in with peers, and trying to make sense of the world and relationships through the immature, cloudy lens of adolescence. Always thinking everyone else has it all sorted and that you are the only one struggling with a sense of identity, the only one lacking in confidence, when in reality we were all paddling as hard as we could, trying not to capsize our individual canoes.

Faraday would now be forever known as 'that place where those kids were taken'. The name 'Faraday' would now evoke feelings of dread and fear and be synonymous with a crime against children. And I was known as one of those girls!

There continued to be a strong press interest in this case for many years, particularly on the anniversary of the crime. Mum would field lots of calls from the press, and if there was a crime in the news involving children, the calls would increase. After the initial furore had died down, Mum was always very reluctant to speak to the press. And as a child growing up with that type of interest, I always thought there was a note of disappointment in the journalist's voices. How did I know that? Well, naturally, I was eavesdropping on the phone calls. When all Mum would say was, 'No comment to make' and 'The children were well and healthy.' This was usually followed by a pregnant pause on the other end, with a journalist saying, 'Oh' in a disappointed tone. 'So, the children are going okay?' They would say, 'So, no mental health issues? Any suicidal tendencies?' in a more hopeful tone.

It didn't help that I was plagued with terrifying nightmares during this time and certain incidents that occurred exacerbated them. Special mention must be made of the escape of both the convicted kidnappers from separate jails, bringing a fresh avalanche of press interest and indeed fear to me that they would try again. It was irrational, but the fear was real.

Robert Clyde Boland escaped from Ararat jail in August 1976, with a fellow prisoner, Peter Rule. They walked to a nearby farm and held up a local farmer and his family, and stole a utility, food, rifle, and ammunition. They abandoned the utility at Gisborne. Apparently, they had run out of fuel.

They then walked quite a distance to Diggers Rest Railway Station, where they threatened the railway station master, Mr Leo Bester, with a rifle and stole his station wagon. Boland pointed the rifle at Mr Bester and said, 'Hand over the keys or I'll blast you.' The police caught up with them a short time later at a petrol station in Footscray. They were filling up the wagon and did not put up any resistance.

Of course, the press reported this incident widely and the Faraday Kidnapping case was brought to the fore again. Mr Rueben Boland (father of Clyde) was reported as saying, 'My son would not have harmed anyone. I told you so. My wife and I are so relieved.' I'm not sure whether Mr Bester or the local farmer and his family would agree.

Edwin John Eastwood escaped from Geelong Prison in December 1976. He remained on the run until 15 February 1977. Eastwood kidnapped another school that was based in Wooreen, Gippsland.

Rob Hunter had been the sole teacher at Wooreen State School 3723 for only nine days. It was his first school since graduating from teachers' college. A very similar presentation to that of Faraday—the children were outside playing at recess when they came running back in to tell Mr Hunter that there was a man outside with a gun.

Mr Hunter was initially unconcerned as he thought it was probably someone out shooting rabbits, but he moved to the door to look outside. He was confronted with a man wearing a balaclava, pointing a gun at his chest. 'Don't try anything fucking smart or I'll shoot you.'

Mr Rob Hunter had the dubious pleasure of meeting an unhinged Eastwood, who had become more violent and erratic. This time he chained the nine children together. There were six girls and three boys, aged from seven to eleven years. One of the little girls asked Eastwood his name and he said, 'Call me Ted.'

I choose not to call him Ted. I always think of him as Eastwood. Calling him Ted awards him with a level of comradeship, even acceptance. He does not deserve that.

Eastwood gagged and blindfolded Rob Hunter, and then took his chain gang of young children and put them in the back of a stolen dodge truck. Rob Hunter was forced onto the passenger side floor. Eastwood then proceeded to yell at the children, telling them to keep down to avoid the flying bullets and if they waved at anyone, he would start shooting.

Eastwood stopped to post a letter at Mirboo North. It was to Minister of Education, Mr Thompson. It contained a crazy ransom note with bizarre demands, which included the release of seventeen of the state's most dangerous criminals, one of which was Robert Clyde Boland. He also wanted large amounts of heroin and cocaine.

Eastwood was driving very erratically with the children in the back and the young male teacher was being thrown around. He took a corner too fast and drove into the back of a logging truck, seriously damaging his stolen vehicle. The two men in the logging truck immediately got out to render assistance and they too were confronted with what they thought was a mad man climbing out the driver's window. He stuck a gun at the head of Mr Robin Smith. Eastwood forced the two men behind the crashed van at gun point. They were chained up behind the truck so no one could see them, but they were very aware of the distressed children in the back of the truck, and a distressed teacher still blindfolded and tied up in the front section. Two more vehicles then pulled up, all to render assistance. Two male truck drivers and two female travellers were too taken hostage and chained up.

Eastwood now had sixteen hostages. He bundled them all in the back of a Kombi van, owned by one of the women, and drove for some time into dense bushland. This was depressingly familiar. Eastwood had a hidden camp site, where he planned to hold his victims for ransom yet again. He chained the male hostages together around a tree, but let the women and children remain unrestrained.

As night fell, Robin Smith slowly worked on the chains around his hands and finally loosened them. At 4.00am, he was able to get his hands free and decided to go for help. Eastwood, at this stage, had just dropped off to sleep. He had set himself up in a banana lounge some distance from the men, supposedly watching them. Mr Smith quietly disengaged himself from the chains and ran for ten kilometres in dense bushland to the nearest farmhouse, where he raised the alarm. The police quickly gathered at the farmhouse and Mr Smith then directed the police back to the camp site to find it abandoned.

In the meantime, Eastwood had woken and realised one of his hostages had escaped. He had nicknamed Mr Smith 'Singlet'. Once realising Singlet had escaped, he became very panicked and forced all the remaining hostages back into the van. It didn't take long for the police to locate the vehicle and a high-speed chase ensured. Eastwood then started shooting at the police out of the driver's window. The police retuned fire and shot out the van tyres and Eastwood, in the ensuing arrest, was shot in the leg. They had caught him again.

Mr Robin Smith was awarded a Commendation for Brave Conduct in 2020 for his actions. He said upon receiving his award, 'I don't consider myself a hero, but I am glad that by doing what I did, everyone got to go home that day. Everyone would have been affected in some way. You can't go through that sort of thing without being affected one way or another. But at least everyone has been able to go on with their lives.'

Mr Robin Smith sounded like a very humble, wise man.

I look at the photo of the Wooreen children with Mr Thompson and Mr Hunter, all smiling broadly after the kidnapping. They had fixed smiles on their faces, so reminiscent of six young girls from Faraday in 1972—them and their young, female teacher, smiling for the press. And my hope is that Mr Smith's wise words have been true for them all.

Again, the press reported this dreadful story widely, and the Faraday Kidnapping was back in the news. Eastwood was not finished yet and was sentenced to a further twenty-one years in prison, which was to be served concurrently with the balance of his sentence from the Faraday Kidnapping. He then went on to strangle and kill convicted rapist, Glen Davies, in the exercise yard of Pentridge Prison in April 1981. He was subsequently acquitted on the grounds of self-defence as he was stabbed ten times in the incident. Not a lot to be proud of.

Each time the convicted kidnappers escaped, a police presence was placed around Mary Gibbs, now Mary Noelker, who was herself a young mother, raising her own family. There were always fears that Mary Noelker would be a target for the convicted kidnappers as she was the outstanding witness for the prosecution. I can only imagine how traumatic and stressful this continual circus being played out in the public arena, with no end in sight, must have been for Mary and her family.

I have no answer to this, but why were both these men able to escape, especially in the same year?

These were men convicted of very serious crimes against children, and once they did escape, they committed even more crimes. It seems very wrong that this was able to occur.

Five years after the kidnapping (in 1977), another incident occurred, which I found disturbing. I was a young teenager. It was winter so it was freezing cold on the farm, and one of my jobs in the evening was to collect sticks and kindling for the wood fires and Mum's wood fire oven. Not one of my favourite jobs. I had embarked on it this particular evening with a lack of enthusiasm. It was drizzling and my hands were really cold. Concentrating on picking up the sticks under the gum trees, I had inadvertently drifted towards the Calder Highway. Usually, I had a circuit I took down near the creek on the north side of our farmhouse (and well away from the highway). It was plentiful in terms of firewood.

I was not taking any notice of the highway or the traffic when something caught my eye. A car had pulled up and parked near our fence, surrounded by long grass. I remember it was a green sedan. A man got out and called out to me, 'Hey you, come over here.' I froze, stood still, looked at the kindling in my arms, then looked towards the man, who appeared to be heading towards the fence, waving at me. This was most odd as our driveway and gate were only fifty metres away to the north, so he wasn't planning on visiting.

I looked around and saw I was alone. Our home was visible, but Mum and my sisters were all inside, and Dad was over at the dairy, milking the cows. I didn't know him, but I felt an overwhelming feeling of dread—a feeling I was beginning to know well. I was scared. I turned for home and started walking slowly, still clutching the kindling. He called out, 'I've got a gun and I'm going to shoot you in your back. Stop and come over here now.' He was shouting now.

All I could think of was, *Not again. And not another man with a gun. What have I done to deserve this?*

Home and safety. I could see our house up on the rise. *One foot in front of the other. Keep walking*, I tell myself. *One step, then the next. Keep walking and don't look back.* I was getting closer to home—and safety! *Keep walking. Why is this happening again?* Then the self-doubt and recriminations in my head started. *It's my fault, I shouldn't have gone near the highway. I never do. What was I thinking? I shouldn't have gone close to the highway.* I never went close to the highway. My thoughts were racing again, but with each step I took, I was certain I would be shot in the back. And it would be the end. *Maybe I am not meant for this world.*

I made it to the rise where our house was located and turned around and looked down on the highway. Both the car and man had gone. I had not heard the car drive away, but I started to shake and vomit. I was concentrating so hard on putting one foot in front of the other. And this experience joined my patchwork of nightmares that would never leave me.

These nightmares always followed a similar pattern— masked men leaning over me, making me feel small and powerless. They were huge and menacing. One had a balaclava over his face. They were both armed. One had a knife. One had a sawn-off rifle. I would usually wake up screaming just as one was about to shoot me. I would wake just as the bullet entered my heart. In some cases, the other man was about to stab me, and I could feel the knife penetrating my heart. The physical symptoms would always consist of heart racing, sweating, eyes unfocused, and the feeling of absolute terror and belief that the two perpetrators were in the room with me, waiting to pounce. I can still smell them. I can still see them.

After one particularly very bad night, where I think I must have woken up nearly the whole house with my screaming, Mum took me to see the local GP in Castlemaine. Mum asked if the nightmares could be connected to the kidnapping, and the GP, an elderly man, looked at me gravely and nodded his head. That was in fact the end of the consultation. After the kidnapping, none of us were offered any counselling or debriefing. It was no one's fault, it was our reality, it was the era we lived in, and the effects of childhood trauma, or *any* form of trauma, were not well researched at that time. My parents, and indeed most of the Howarths, were a very stoic bunch. You dealt with what life dished out to you. You moved on, tried not to think about it, and you tried not to show any emotion or vulnerability. It wasn't the healthiest way of dealing with trauma, or life in general, but it was the only strategy we had at the time.

51

Adulting

It was a relief to leave adolescence behind, make my way into the world as an adult and embark on a nursing career.

I like to think I am a kind, competent, hardworking nurse, but at the beginning of my career, I wasn't confident and I was inept. As a young nursing student in Bendigo, I was careful not to mention that I came from Faraday, as I never wanted to draw any attention to myself. I was mortified when I was cruelly taunted by a nursing tutor. She somehow knew my history and singled me out in a psychiatric nursing tutorial. She was actually the psychiatric nurse tutor, which made her actions even more bizarre. I was a quiet, average student, who rarely asked a question in class and generally tried to make myself invisible. At our second tutorial for this subject, I was aware that this tutor was staring at me in an unfriendly manner and was taken aback when this female tutor, who I did not know, called me by name, loudly, and started with, 'Now, Robyn …' She said it in a jocular tone and then continued with, 'You come from Faraday, don't you?' Startled and embarrassed, I replied that I did. This was most peculiar as it was not in context with the lesson plan.

I wondered where this was going. She continued, her voice becoming louder, making sure to make me the centre of attention. With all eyes in the class now firmly on me, she said, 'So, you were part of the kidnapping there, weren't you?' With eyes averted, face turning bright red and my head down, I mumbled that I was. Blind Freddy would have been able to see that I was clearly very uncomfortable with this exchange. But it got worse. 'Oh, come on. Tell us all about it.' She called out in glee in front of the whole class, 'It wasn't that bad. It was just a bit of a picnic, wasn't it? They never hurt you at all, and you probably got paid a lot of money for all those photos in the newspapers. You and your family loved the publicity, didn't you? You chased the publicity, didn't you?' And then her tone became very nasty. I froze then, as this seemed like a really personal attack. I really couldn't answer in any coherent manner except to mumble that I didn't really want to talk about it. She continued in a similar vein, gleefully taunting me and insinuating that it was all a big fuss over nothing. I sat there wishing the floor would swallow me up. My head was down but I did notice quite a few of my nursing colleagues looking very uncomfortable and shooting sympathetic glances my way.

I have often wondered what her rationale was as one would have thought that a nurse trained in the psychiatric field would have some understanding, or even empathy. But instead, she appeared to get some sort of perverse enjoyment out of taunting a student, who had experienced a major childhood trauma, in a very personal manner.

This exchange worsened my insomnia. I was living in a share house in Bendigo with three other young nurses and I was generally enjoying life. They were great girls to share a house with as we had a lot in common, all being from rural Victoria.

On their days off, they would return to their family homes in Nullawil, Pyramid Hill and Heathcote. And on my days off, I would always return home to Faraday. I was too embarrassed to tell them, or anyone really, but if I was to spend a night in the house on my own, I would be terrified and would average one hour sleep per night. I would usually get to sleep at 5.00 am and have to be up at 6.00 am for an early shift. I would go to work exhausted.

Those nights on my own, I would lie in bed, frozen with fear, heart racing, mouth dry, staring at the bedroom window, which faced out towards the road.

I was certain I could hear footsteps outside, certain that any minute I would hear the windowpane unlatch, I would see the windowpane slowly move upwards, and a balaclava-covered man would climb through the window. In the end, I gave up trying to spend a night on my own. It was easier to drive home to the farm in Faraday.

I remember often working until 11.00 pm in Bendigo, then driving home to the farm in Faraday, getting to bed at midnight. I would start the next day at 5.30 am and return to Bendigo in time for a 7.00 am start. I figured five hours sleep was better than no sleep. It would be many years to come before I could spend a night in my home alone and feel safe.

As a teenager and young adult, I rarely told anyone where I was from as I did not want to answer questions about the kidnapping. On occasion, when meeting new people who were aware of my history, my heart would always sink when, with a gleam in their eye, they would ask, 'And are you one of those girls? Ooohhh, tell us all about it.' I was so tired of it all. I was so very tired.

For Mum, the trauma was deep-seated and never spoken about. She shuddered at the mention of Faraday and once, in more recent years, she was invited to attend a CWA function that was to be held at the Faraday school, now a private residence. But she could not bring herself to attend. Mum never talked about the events of 6 October 1972, but she painstakingly cut out every press clipping on the kidnapping over many years and pasted them in a large book, which she later entrusted into my safekeeping.

The press has now given up on ringing her. But for many years they would always, on the anniversary of the crime, request a photo, and each time they did she would always refuse.

The one time she did weaken, and it was against her better judgement, was approximately three years after the kidnapping. A photo was taken and appeared on the front page of the *Herald Sun*. It had an accompanying story titled, 'Faraday three years onwards.'

On Thursday of that week, Mum went to Castlemaine on her usual weekly shopping trip and entered one of the local stores, where two women were speaking quite loudly. As she took her place in line behind them, they glanced behind at Mum and continued their conversation. 'Did you see the front page of *the Sun?*' the portly, middle-aged women remarked to her smaller-built friend. Her friend replied, 'Yes, I did! It's disgraceful the way those parents are chasing the publicity. You know, I heard those Howarths, the ones with the three daughters involved, have made a pretty penny out of this.' The first woman exclaimed, 'You know, I have heard that as well. It would almost be worth having your kids kidnapped. You know they get paid every time their photos appear in the newspaper?'

'Hmph!' snorted her friend, 'And we know how often that is.' In a very nasty tone, the woman responded with, 'Just disgusting.'

Mum, a very private, shy woman at the best of times, and also a young mother, who had gone through the most unimaginable trauma—one that no mother should ever have to go through—was horrified. She was horrified that people were talking about us again, and horrified and gutted to think that people would think that, as our parents, they were somehow profiting from this crime. Of course, they never did. Mum backed out of the shop without even starting her shopping. Feeling very upset, she burst into tears when she got home and told Dad all about it. Dad told her that they were just jealous *they* didn't get their photos in the paper.

I generally love rural communities and have seen firsthand the wonderful support, care and kindness that was shown to us in the aftermath of the kidnapping. However, I have also seen how people are treated if they are a little different or do not quite fit in—or like in our case, they garner a lot of publicity for a crime they would never have chosen to be a part of. Rural communities act as a magnifying glass for life. They can shine a spotlight, showcasing people working together and being there for each other in hardship and crisis, and provide a sense of identity and belonging. But on the other hand, they magnify injustice, malice and exclusion, which is often very present in small communities. It is soul destroying for those who do not quite fit in or are a little different. I have always believed those two women in that shop knew Mum was standing behind them—such cruel and malicious behaviour.

Aah, rural communities. So much to love about them, but on the other hand so much to hate about them.

52
Madness and mothering

The years went by and I married, changed my name, and moved away from that beautiful hamlet called Faraday. I reinvented myself and was no longer known as 'one of those girls'. In my twenties and early thirties, I was blessed to have three healthy children, all now adults, who gave me great joy as babies, toddlers and children. But there were some days when I thought I was going mad, terrified that one night a masked man with a knife would climb though my children's bedroom window and steal them away. I would not be able to bear it. These thoughts would not leave me.

I became quite unwell after the birth of my third baby. I had a mixture of postnatal depression and untreated post-traumatic stress disorder (PTSD). It was ironic really, but the trigger that sent me into a serious mental health decline, was sending my little girl, my eldest child, to primary school. I lived in a rural community that I was very happy with and elected to send her to the local primary school. She happily started school, but my feelings of dread and disquiet grew as I kept having these crazy thoughts that my little girl was not safe at school. I would find myself dropping her off at school, she would happily run in, and then I would continually drive around the school grounds with a toddler and newborn baby in the back seat, obsessively searching for men wearing balaclavas, convinced that an intruder was going to break into the school grounds at any minute.

At night I would prowl around my childrens' bedrooms, obsessively checking that all the windows were closed and locked, and *double* checking that all doors were locked. I would get to bed then quickly jump out again to do one more nightly check, and then another, and then another. Sleep was hard to come by.

It all came crashing down on me one day when I sat at the breakfast table and just stared at my three children. I had gone down a very dark tunnel, and all I could see was blackness. All of a sudden, I had a packet of cornflakes in my hand and had no idea how to pour the cereal into the breakfast bowls. The children's voices were growing fainter and fainter as they were calling out, 'Mum. Mum, we are hungry.' I could no longer function. I phoned home expecting to speak to Mum and got Dad, which was unusual. Mum was down at the church fellowship at Harcourt, having morning tea. I remember saying to Dad, 'I'm in trouble, Dad. I can't feed the kids breakfast.' Dad, in true Howarth fashion, said, 'What do you mean you can't feed the kids breakfast? How bloody hard is it to feed the kids breakfast?' With that, I burst into tears and yelled at him, 'You just don't get it. I'm in serious trouble,' and I hung up the phone.

I would later learn that Dad drove the farm ute down to Harcourt Church in his farm clothes and rubber boots, border collie onboard, and ran into the church fellowship group. He interrupted morning tea, bellowing at Mum, 'Robyn's in trouble. You have got to go to her quick smart.' I lived several hours away. I have often wondered what the ladies at the church fellowship thought that morning.

Mum came to stay, the children got fed and I got medicated.

My emotional health had deteriorated. My illogical thoughts were taking over my days and my newborn baby was unsettled and slept very little. The combination of maternal exhaustion and stress forced me to face my demons and seek long overdue counselling.

The first counselling session went very well. I found it liberating to finally speak freely about the kidnapping and how it had made me feel, and that deep down I was scared and angry and I was tired of feeling that way. The counsellor's name was Clare. She was very kind and concerned, but also very shocked that we had never received any counselling or assistance from the Victims of Crime service. Of course, we never thought to ask for any.

After our first session, Clare asked me to go home and write down how I was feeling about the kidnapping. The next day I sat at the kitchen table, pen and paper in hand, and stared at the pad. I wrote nothing. I just couldn't do it. I cancelled the second session, left a voice message saying I was fine now and thanked Clare for her time.

After Clare retrieved my phone message from her answering machine, she phoned me at home that evening, and urged me to reconsider counselling. She gently told me that I did not have to continue with her, but I did need to see someone as I couldn't keep suppressing long pent-up feelings that were making me ill. As a true Howarth, I decided I really didn't need to do it and would revert to our usual ways of coping, which was burying our feelings so deep that they manifested in different ways—usually ill health. But I pondered on that conversation and decided to keep the next appointment. And with Clare's encouragement, I started writing. What I wrote did not make a lot of sense. There was no punctuation and words ran into each other, but soon a torrent of words appeared, page after page. It was as if Clare had given me permission to write my truth.

I finally realised I was terrified of writing it all down because I was angry. Angry with the police for making me go through the line-up. Angry with the court system. Angry with the press. And deep down, I was angry with myself. I should have been braver. I should have been able to help better, to kick out the back of the van. And I shouldn't be angry as I was one of the lucky ones—I had survived and so many hadn't.

Then there's the guilt. The stories of the Beaumont children, Joanne Ratcliffe, Kriste Gordon, Karmein Chan, and Graeme Thorne—the children who never got to come home. Just a few of many. They have always haunted me. And deep down I felt guilty that I had survived, when so many others had not.

Spending time with a counsellor, who was skilled, emphatic and safe, helped me to make sense of my illogical thoughts and see them for what they were—a post-traumatic stress response to a major childhood trauma. It wasn't that I was losing my mind. Clare described the trauma as imagining I have a scar, and every now and then something will irritate it. The scar then will become inflamed and I will be aware of it.

She said this is the time to take stock, check the scar, see if it is inflamed, angry and red, and really think about, and reflect honestly, about what has caused it. It is a time to acknowledge that sometimes there are good reasons for the scar becoming irritated and as it continues to heal, the irritation will become less and less. But in times when the scar is burning hot, that is the time for some serious self-care. This analogy has really helped me. There have been many times over the years when my scar has been red hot, and each time, I ignored the Howarth motto and took myself off to see many psychologists and counsellors, who all helped to bring compassion—and often clarity—to my thoughts.

One such man, David Jones in Shepparton, was such a kind and wise psychologist. He helped me so much in the midst of the breakdown of my first marriage, and for some years after I would regularly obtain my mental health plan from a random GP and book in for my sessions with David. He always listened without judgement and gave wise counsel, and I always looked forward to our sessions. I think he did as well as we developed a warm comradery.

One such time was when I just felt in need of an emotional tune up as visions of the kidnapping had been preying on my mind, but with no apparent triggers. I started seeing David again and mused that one day I should write this story for my children and, at that stage, future grandchildren. I ended our session with a flippant comment, saying, 'Well, just as well the kidnappers were so inept as I sit here before you alive, hale and hearty, able to talk freely with you.' David, who was a man in his sixties, was grey haired and wore glasses, and he had a very kind smile. He sat quietly for a moment, glasses perched on the bridge of his nose. He then peered over them and looked at me with concern.

He said, in a grave voice, 'Have you never thought that because they were so inept, that actually put you in much greater danger, because if challenged, or the teacher or yourselves became hysterical, there was a very good chance they would have lost control?' We both sat in silence for a moment and his comments gave me cause to reflect, as I had never thought about it quite like that.

I had always carried the belief that they did indeed plan to murder us, but when faced with the reality of doing so, they could not go through with it. That belief always gave me some small comfort, but after speaking to David, the realisation hit me on just how perilous our situation truly was.

53

Finding peace and wisdom

The decades passed, I reclaimed my maiden name and became a grandmother. My parents departed this earth and the circle of life continues.

Dad, after years of ill health, died at age sixty–nine. He suffered with rheumatoid arthritis, which was not helped with the hard manual labour required to run the farm. Auntie June always said, 'Dad's health worsened significantly after the events of 1972.' And it was hard to watch his physical decline.

Mum lived to the ripe old age of eighty–five. She never spoke about the kidnapping or the effects on her, but as she slipped into dementia, some days she would get a faraway look on her face, a worried frown would appear and she would say to us (often), 'You are all right, aren't you? They didn't hurt you, did they?'

I remain in awe of the bravery and sheer nerve of a young twenty-year-old teacher named Mary Gibbs. How do you ever thank someone for being so brave? A first-year teacher, a small, petite woman, who stood firm in the face of a menace and did not flinch in protecting her charges. It should have been the most one-sided of contests. On one side, two adult men armed with guns, knives and chains, and a grandiose plan of evil greed. On the other side, six small girls and a young woman with kick-arse boots and the prayers of a nation.

We owe Mary Gibbs our lives.

We also owe a huge debt of gratitude to Deputy Premier and Minister of Education, Lindsay Thompson, who put his own life on the line in Woodend that fateful night to deliver the ransom money. He was very brave and remained concerned for the fate of all the children involved in both the Faraday and Wooreen kidnappings for years to come.

The Victorian Police force, and in particular, Reg Baker. The gods were looking out for us when they assigned Reg to our case.

And to six little girls, who overcame major childhood trauma and went on to all lead very happy and successful lives in their chosen fields. We did good.

54
Today. Castlemaine.

The locals still speak of the 'Faraday Kidnapping' in hushed tones. They can recount exactly what they were doing that night, even though it is over fifty years ago. Many were helping with the search for six little girls and a young, pretty, first-year teacher. Some were trying to organise a whip around to try and help raise the ransom money. Many, I suspect, spent time looking at their own sleeping children and thought, *Thank God, not my children*. But in many ways, we became their children. We became the community's children. I returned to live in Castlemaine for a short time some years ago, and I was very taken aback by the narrative around the Faraday Kidnapping. It had almost become folklore. Friends of my parents would stop me in the street and tell me how good it was to see that I had come home, and then they would gently squeeze my hand and say quietly, 'I searched for you that night.' I would then get quite teary and simply say, 'Thank you.'

During this time in Castlemaine, I remember clearly being invited out to spend an evening with friends at Sutton Grange, a rural farming area on the other side of Mt Alexander, but very near to Faraday. Sitting around a campfire with great company, enjoying a glass of red wine, we all started sharing stories of where we grew up. These were new friends, and I gave a vague response that I grew up on the other side of Mount Alexander on a farm and had recently returned to the area after a long time away. (Old habits die hard). One of the men piped up and said, 'That would be near Faraday, wouldn't it? Of course. You are much too young to be involved in that dreadful bloody history. But just thinking about those kids being taken, it has always scared the bejeesus out of me.' I gave a rueful smile at being thought too young to be involved and agreed that the story had always scared the bejeesus out of me as well.

We were not rich. We were not famous. We did not live in the fast lane. We simply went to school one day and men with evil and greed on their mind came for us. This could have happened to anyone, and that struck fear and uncertainty into the very heart of the community and society as we knew it then. Our way of life had been threatened and the community responded with fury.

The nightmares have left me and I now sleep very well at night. My scar has healed but can, at times, become irritated. But I am at peace with that now.

A lot of reflection and lots of tears have gone into writing this story. My words are clumsy, my writing skills are not fluid and professional, but throughout this process I believe I have found my voice and a deeper understanding of what I actually want to convey.

I hope I will be brave enough to get this story published. And I hope that just maybe it may bring some comfort to those who have experienced childhood trauma or have been a victim of a crime. Recovery *is* possible.

I really do not like the term 'victims' because we are *survivors*.

When I think of Faraday now, I no longer think of guns, balaclava-clad men with knives, and dug-out trenches. I think of family and belonging. I think of a beautiful blue stone school building, where the community once gathered with pride. I think of Border Leicester sheep, with some very fine wool, that won first prize at the Castlemaine Show. I think of the most delicious apples in the world—from our very own orchard—and sweet mulberries from Grandma's garden. I think of Sunday roasts cooked on the wood oven, with roast potatoes roasting in the juices of the store bought roast lamb. I think of border collie dogs that all eventually put up with Dad's idea of sheep dog training.

I think of the rolling hills, still part of the original Howarth holdings, which I now own jointly with my sister. I think of the panoramic views of Mount Alexander and Mount Macedon, home to hundreds of free-range kangaroos and one koala. When I walk those hills at Faraday, it brings me such peace, and I reflect on the rich friendships from my school days that still endure to this day. I think of school sports and fabulous Christmas concerts.

For many years, I thought the community of Faraday was lost after 1972, but I now realise that I have always carried it with me. It remains an integral part of my childhood and the values of resilience and decency have sustained me over my lifetime.

And finally—a long overdue acknowledgement:

I come from a beautiful little hamlet called Faraday. I went to Faraday State School No. 797. It educated me well, as it did my father, and his father before him. Faraday was our home. It was our community. It was our school. And it was always, and still is, so much more than a kidnapping.

My name is Robyn Howarth and I am very proud to say I come from Faraday.

End Note

In the aftermath of this crime, there were some interesting outcomes:

- Mary Gibbs was awarded the George Medal for bravery (Jan 1973)

This is the highest recognition of civilian valour awarded in Britain and the Commonwealth.

The announcement read that Gibbs displayed courage, coolness and initiative of a high order and by her example and leadership, she kept the spirts of the children high.

- Assistant Commissioner Crowley was awarded a Queen's Police Medal.
- Assistant Commissioner Mick Miller went onto become the police commissioner.
- Senior Sergeant Reginald George Baker would go on to become an assistant commissioner and his investigation and subsequent interview of Edwin John Eastwood would be used as a teaching tool for junior police officers.

END NOTE

- Dad was a lifelong fan of Senior Sergeant Reginald Baker.
- Mr Lindsay Thompson received a bravery award and became Premier of Victoria.
- Mrs Kit Chapman was awarded a British Empire Medal for manning the CFA channels for seventy-two hours with no sleep, to ensure vital communications were able to keep transmitting.

Notes on Sources

Day 9 at Wooreen By Rob Hunter
Reg Baker's memoirs
Robyn Howarth's memories
Iris Howarth's collection of press articles for many decades

Supreme Court of Victoria
R V Boland appeal (1974)
Wayne Grant
The Sun Magazine 1975

Appendix

Miss Mary Gibbs, aged twenty years (transcript of evidence, *Herald Sun*, Nov 1972)

At 1.35 whilst playing musical chairs two men burst through the door, there were two doors and they came though part of the wire door. They just charged in and said, 'Schools over for the day.' One man had a sawn off shot gun and he was also carrying a brown bag and wearing a grey, khaki balaclava. The second man had a funny sort of cloth hat and glasses on. I was sitting on my chair. They came to me and told the children to go and stand near their desks. I said to them, 'We haven't got anything for you to take,' and they said, 'They didn't want money.' I said, 'What do you want? There is nothing here for you,' and they said, 'You are worth a million dollars to us.' I think it was the older man who said that. Neither explained what they meant. After that I got a little hysterical and started to cry a bit and the man with the gun herded the children out. I didn't know where he was taking them and I was left with the older man. The older man kept saying that everything would be alright, not to worry it would be alright. I said, 'You are not going to hurt us, are you? We are all girls. You are not going to touch us?' He said not to worry about it. The younger man then came back in and told us to hurry up and I said, 'What about if we don't go with you?' He opened up a bag full of chains and padlocks and things and said, 'We will use these.'

Miss Gibbs said she then got up and went to the door and the man with the gun went to the telephone and did something to the phone. She was ushered into the back of the van, and the younger man put the gun in an overnight bag. The younger man then went back into the school and the older man said he was going to leave something in a table drawer so people would know what had happened. The young teacher asked if it could be left out where it could be found easier. There was no reply.

He then said, 'It was for a million dollars from Mr Thompson, being the minister for education.' Miss Gibbs said that while travelling in the van with the younger man, she again asked about the note. She said the younger man told her again, 'It is for one million dollars from Mr Thompson, because he is the education minister. They will have to pay as it is election year.'

www.ingramcontent.com/pod-product-compliance
Ingram Content Group UK Ltd.
Pitfield, Milton Keynes, MK11 3LW, UK
UKHW061223180426